Stressbusters

Happy
Easter
2019!
Love,
Vicki

Stressbusters

For Teens Under Pressure

STEVE SHORES

SERVANT PUBLICATIONS
ANN ARBOR, MICHIGAN

Vine Books is an imprint of Servant Publications especially designed to serve evangelical Christians.

Servant Publications—Mission Statement
We are dedicated to publishing books that spread the gospel of Jesus Christ, help Christians to live in accordance with that gospel, promote renewal in the church, and bear witness to Christian unity.

Scripture quotes labeled THE MESSAGE are taken from THE MESSAGE. Copyright by Eugene H. Peterson 1993, 1994, 1995. Used by permission of NavPress Publishing Group. Scripture quotes labeled NASB are from the New American Standard Bible, copyright The Lockman Foundation 1960, 1962, 1963, 1968, 1971, 1972, 1973, 1975, 1977. Scripture quotes labeled NIV are taken from the HOLY BIBLE, NEW INTERNATIONAL VERSION®. Copyright 1973, 1978, 1984 by International Bible Society. Used by permission of Zondervan Publishing House. All rights reserved. Scripture quotations marked NKJV are from the New King James Version, copyright 1979, 1980, 1982, Thomas Nelson, Inc., Publishers. Scripture quotes labeled KJV are from the King James Version.

Servant Publications
P.O. Box 8617
Ann Arbor, MI 48107
www.servantpub.com

Cover design by Uttley/Douponce DesignWorks, Sisters, Oregon

02 03 04 05 10 9 8 7 6 5 4 3 2 1

Printed in the United States of America
ISBN 1-56955-312-2

Library of Congress Cataloging-in-Publication Data

Shores, Steve.
  Stressbusters : for teens under pressure / Steve Shores.
      p. cm.
Includes bibliographical references.
  ISBN 1-56955-312-2
  1. Stress in adolescence–Juvenile literature. 2. Stress management
for teenagers–Juvenile literature. I. Title.
  BF724.3.S86 S56 2002
  155.9'042–dc21

2002008511

Contents

Welcome to the Wonderful World of Stress

Heidi, a fourteen-year-old freshman, has just transferred to a new school, almost a thousand miles away from her old hometown. It's hard enough to face the challenges of high school for the first time. But Heidi has to do it alone, in a totally unfamiliar city—without the support of people she's known her whole life. Heidi misses her old friends—and she worries that she doesn't have the right clothes, looks, or personality to make new ones. Is she doomed to spend the next four years as an outcast?

Drew, an outgoing high school junior, has always done pretty well in school. But this year, he's struggled with grades for the first time. For one thing, the course work is harder. (His parents insisted that he take several advanced classes to help prepare him for college.) He's also working part time as a courtesy clerk at the local grocery store, so he can fill up his old Volkswagen with gas and pay his share of the car insurance. But now, his grades are slipping—and his latest report card carries an ominous message to his parents: "Drew is very intelligent, but is not living up to his potential." Drew worries what will happen when his parents read the note. *Will Mom and Dad make me quit my job? Am I going to have to give up my car—and my freedom?*

Stephanie, a sensitive seventeen-year-old, is what you might call a "late bloomer." All throughout high school, the guys have treated her like a little sister; no one has shown even the slightest romantic interest. Until recently, she'd never been asked on a single date—something she's felt pretty embarrassed about. (She doesn't know that that's pretty normal.) But yesterday, a gorgeous guy from the basketball team invited Stephanie to the prom. The problem is, this guy has a reputation for sleeping around. Thrilled that she had been asked (finally!), Stephanie said she'd love to go. But now she's worried about what he'll expect from her on prom night and about what other people will think. Should she back out, try talking to him about the situation beforehand, or just go to the prom and hope for the best? Like Heidi and Drew, Stephanie is seriously *stressed.*

Welcome to the Stress Zone

Maybe you're not starting a new school, facing a bad report card, or worried about your prom date. But in one way or another, you're feeling stress about something. Why am I so sure? It's simple. *Stress happens.* It's all a part of being alive. If you've got a pulse, you've got stress. If you're able to read this book, you're facing it just like all the rest of us.

I don't have to tell *you* that the teen years are stressful—you're living them. By now, you've probably guessed that the teen years are among the most stress-filled times in your life. Not convinced? Take a look at this list of possible stressors, and mark the ones that you're dealing with ... just this week!

- getting into college
- paying for college
- starting to date
- never getting a date
- asking someone for a date
- getting your homework done
- taking tests
- taking your PSATs/SATs or ACTs
- facing a misunderstanding with your friend(s)
- ending friendships/making new ones
- fitting in at school
- pressure to have sex
- struggling with the urge to have sex
- getting pregnant (or getting someone pregnant) after having sex
- tension between you and your mom or dad (or a brother or sister)
- needing money
- your parents needing more money
- dysfunctional family issues: divorced parents, alcoholic parent, or abusive family situation (physical, sexual, verbal, or emotional abuse)
- blended family (getting to know a new step-parent or step-siblings)
- weight issues (feeling too fat or too thin, dealing with bulimia, anorexia, or compulsive eating)
- getting onto a sports team (or playing well on the team you're already on)
- pressure to take drugs

- pressure to sell drugs
- pressure to party/get drunk
- not getting invited to a party (or parties)
- being seen as a nerd
- being seen as "easy"
- school violence
- facing a new school/new classes
- getting a new teacher (or coach)
- embarrassment about your physical development (either you're way ahead of or way behind your peers)
- humiliation over major acne (or other physical stressor)
- fighting parents
- illness in the family
- death of a grandparent
- death of a friend (from illness, suicide, anorexia, drunk driving accident, or any other cause)
- getting good grades
- trying to find time for schoolwork, social life, jobs, family relationships, chores, and hobbies
- sick pet
- living up to others' expectations (parents, teachers, friends, boss, coach, and others)
- trying to establish independence from your parents
- trying to figure out what you want to do when you graduate
- just plain growing up

Those are just a *few* of the stressors that teens face on a regular basis. If you sat down and made a list, you could probably make one three times as long. In fact, you're going to have a chance to do that in just a minute (though your list doesn't really have to be that lengthy). But first, let me explain exactly what I mean when I talk about "stress" and "stressors."

STRESS 101:

What is "stress" anyway? Basically, "stress" is your body's reactions to the challenges you face in your daily life (at school, work, home, etc.), and "stressors" are those challenges that cause the stress. Luckily, not all stress is bad. We all need to be stimulated by things that cause us to learn and grow. Years ago, a guy named Hans Selye (a Canadian researcher known as "the father of modern stress research") said: "Stress is not even necessarily bad for you. It is also the spice of life."

All right, then. Spice is good! On the other hand, stress can also hurt us—especially if it goes on for too long, or if we don't have healthy, constructive ways of dealing with it. But you *can* do things to lower your stress level—and help you enjoy yourself more.

STRESSBUSTER:

What are the things that are stressing you out the most? Get out your journal or a notebook that you can use while reading this book. Now make a list of those things that are really causing stress in your life. Add things to this list in the days and weeks ahead as we talk about the causes and results of stress.

After you've made your list, put stars or check marks next to the three things that are stressing you the most right now. Try to answer this question: "Why are these areas particularly stressful for me?"

Gone are the days when a teen might come home from school and complain, "The teacher made me put my gum on my nose when I got caught chewing it in class." If only that was the worst thing teens had to worry about! Now, it's more like: "The security officer made us go through the metal detector twice, because a kid smuggled a knife into school yesterday."

What a quantum leap in stress points! How can teens deal with this increase in stress, especially when families—which used to be our refuge in stress storms—are more and more likely to be stressful places themselves?

Stress comes from a lot of places. But for many of us, stress comes from the feeling that the resources we have are not enough to meet all the demands we face. We don't feel that we're good enough, smart enough, popular enough, loved enough, talented enough, or even just well-slept enough to face the challenges ahead.

Sound familiar? You're not alone. The good news is you have a lot more going for you than you realize. This book will help you find those resources and use them in ways that will give you a better, healthier, and less stressed life.

Fuel for the Journey

Whenever you want to go somewhere in your car, you need to fill up with gas. Without fuel, the car just won't move.

In the same way, whenever you want to get somewhere in life, you need to get "gas" for the journey. That's what we're going to focus on in the first half of this book. You are the car. Your resources are the gas. We'll work on increasing your resources, or getting you more of what you need so that you can get where you want in life.

In the second half of *Stressbusters,* we'll take a closer look at some of the specific stresses you and your friends may be facing and explore how you can manage those endless demands. Along the way, we'll give your life a tuneup, so that it won't be filled with so much stress and, as a result, use up all the precious fuel you already have in your tank.

So let's get started. Don't stress out! What's ahead will be pretty painless, and hopefully a lot of fun. Best of all, it'll help you bring your stress back under control so that you can enjoy the kind of low-stress, confident life you want to live.

ONE

Connecting With God

There's no question in Tyler's mind what his biggest stressor is. During his first two years of high school, he played freshman and junior varsity football and dreamed of the day he'd get to play at the varsity level. This year, he's finally playing on the varsity team.

At first, he had a *blast*. But now, a few weeks into practice, things aren't going so well. Anyone who's played football (or any other sport) knows coaches can be great, but some can be a real pain. This year, Tyler is especially unlucky, because his head coach is a particularly cranky guy. And, for reasons Tyler doesn't understand, the coach is acting like *Tyler* is the major source of his problems.

Since the beginning of the year, the coach has made it clear that he doesn't like Tyler—and every week it's gotten worse. The other day, after Tyler fumbled the ball, the coach ran up to him on the field, grabbed him by the bars on the front of his helmet, and screamed at him until spittle formed in the corners of the coach's mouth.

What was Tyler's reaction to this crazy man? Naturally, he was embarrassed to be treated that way in front of his teammates. He also wondered: What did I do that was so bad? Do I really stink as a player? Is there something wrong with me? Voices inside Tyler's head started to whisper, *Well, the coach wouldn't act that way unless you deserve it! Now everyone's going to know the truth—you're no good. You shouldn't even be on the team!*

Beneath those voices, though, were other voices—quiet, but firm voices telling him: *This guy doesn't know what he's talking about. Don't let him bother you. You belong on this team.* Clearest of all was the voice inside him shouting, *Get away from this jerk!* Tyler knows he needs to stay out of the line of fire. He wants to put as much distance as possible between himself and the coach.

Why? Because he wasn't made to be the target of someone else's contempt or out-of-control anger. And neither were you. In his gut, Tyler knows his coach's yelling went beyond anything he should be expected to put up with. He understands that he's dealing with someone who not only isn't especially good for him, but who could possibly do real harm.

STRESS 101:

Why is stress so bad? When you experience too much stress, for too long, it can make you feel unhappy, angry, depressed, and anxious. It may make you cranky, and it may make you cry. More than that, it can actually make you physically ill. Some symptoms of stress that you may have experienced are:

- heart beating faster
- rapid breathing
- headaches
- stomachaches
- sweating
- sleeplessness
- chest pains

- prolonged illness/getting sick all the time
- diarrhea
- acne breakouts

Yuk! Being a teenager is challenging enough without dealing with all this stuff. You can do things to lower your stress level, though, and we'll talk about that in the chapters ahead.

The Voices of Stress

We all hear voices in our lives—some real, some imagined. Many of the voices come from our parents, our teachers, and other adults. Some are the voices of our friends. Still others are those "voices-that-aren't-exactly-voices" we all hear in our heads. Sometimes these voices tell us how great we are. But much more often, it seems, they tear us down.

What did you do that for? Now everyone will know how stupid you are!

You're such a loser!

If you can't do it right, doofus, don't even try.

These voices make us feel small and worthless. They tell us that we don't matter, that we won't ever be good at anything, that we've made a total mess of our lives. These voices are loud and steady and hard to ignore.

They're also dead wrong.

Best of all, they have no real power. God made you, and he loves you. He designed you to receive his love. It was never his plan for you to listen to these voices. God is forever saying wonderful things about those he loves. (That's you.) His voice is the one voice that is *always* worth listening to.

To Jesus, you're the best part of the food—the spice that makes it taste good. In other words, you're the salt on his fries. You're the dip on his chip. You're the cream inside his Hostess cupcake. Okay. You get it. You're *valuable* to him. This is what God wants you to understand about yourself.

STRESSBUSTER:

Take out your journal and open it to a new page. Divide it into two columns. In the first column, write down a list of ten good things about yourself. What do you like about yourself? What do you think God likes about you? What would your friends say if someone asked them to describe you? What are some of your unique talents and gifts?

In the second column, write down some of the negative messages you get from those voices in your head, or from parents, coaches, teachers, or other teens.

Now, write the heading "Truths" over the first column, and "Lies" over the second.

Finally, go back to the first column, and write an answer to each of the "Lies" in the second column. For example, if you wrote "I'm stupid," now write: "I'm very smart." If you wrote "I'm a loser," put "I have good gifts and abilities!" in the first column. It may sound stupid, but how are you ever going to believe it if you don't hear it? Having a positive attitude can help you beat stress. Best of all, it can help you to become the person you were meant to be—and to recognize how wonderful you already are (even if you don't know it yet!).

Good Voices v. Bad Voices

Somewhere in your life, there's someone who's telling you good things about yourself and your life. Maybe it's your youth leader. Maybe a sister or brother. Maybe your mom or dad, or your best friend. That's great. Treasure those voices. But no matter who else you've got, there's always God himself. (If you want proof, try reading a page or so of your Bible each night. You'll be surprised at all the encouraging stuff you can find in there!)

God wants us to hear the good things he and the people who love us have to say. But if we listen too much to the negative voices, the ones that drag us down, it gets harder and harder to hear anything encouraging or hopeful.

Don't believe me? Think for a minute about how hard it is for most people to take a compliment. How do you respond when someone says, "You look great today" or "You're an incredible ball player!"? If you're like most people, you probably say something like, "Are you kidding? I look terrible!" or "Nah, I'm not nearly as good as Steve." We ignore the positive feedback we get, focusing instead on all the negative stuff, including all our (real or imagined) faults and flaws.

STRESSBUSTER:

Do you have trouble accepting compliments? Practice these answers out loud—and promise yourself that you'll use one of them the next time someone praises you!

- "That's really nice of you to say!"
- "Aww! I love your dress (haircut, shoes, necklace, etc.), too!"
- "You are so sweet!"
- "That means a lot to me, coming from you."
  —and, the most radical answer of all—
- "Thank you!"

Don't worry about sounding dorky. Practice this when no one else is around. It really does help.

Still feel uncomfortable? That's okay. Use those feelings to help you figure out what's going on inside. Do you feel funny because you're talking to yourself? (A perfectly reasonable reaction.) Or does it feel strange to compliment yourself? Is it awkward for you to accept compliments from *anyone?* Think about why, and resolve to be more open in this area. You deserve to hear and believe those good words!

When our heads fill up with nagging voices, we naturally want to run away from them—just like Tyler wanted to get away from Coach Spittle-Mouth. But the problem is, a lot of times we don't know where we can get away *to*. We tune out one negative voice, only to find ourselves listening to another just like it—or worse. A guy who tries to escape the voice of a parent demanding high grades might be influenced instead by friends who say he should be "scoring" with his girlfriend. A girl who's told by an insensitive friend that her backside looks big might become obsessed with a voice that tells her to starve herself down to the "perfect" (and deadly) weight of 100 pounds.

The thing about these other voices is, a lot of times they sound like they know what they're talking about. Sex, drugs, popularity, good grades, money, cars, a boyfriend or girlfriend, and lots of other things can sound like the answers to our problems. How can we know if they are—or if they aren't? You and I both know, sometimes it's just not that clear.

Head North

Stuart was part of a group of guys who loved to camp. In fact, several of his friends had been Boy Scouts and loved nothing more than to go out in the woods and "rough it" for the weekend.

This year, for spring break, the guys decided to head off to the Wallowa Mountains, a couple of hours from their home in eastern Oregon. Stuart was in charge of bringing the food. Several of his friends were responsible for planning their route and choosing their campsites.

The first day and night, everything went according to plan. The weather was awesome. The trails were nearly empty. Stuart felt like he was on a real adventure. He was so glad his friends had asked him to come along. This was the trip of a lifetime!

The next day, around midafternoon, the guys decided to step off of the trail—just about fifty feet or so. They wanted to get up on a higher ridge, to see if they could get a better view. They could. It was incredible!

But when they tried to make their way back to the trail, they got turned around. After hiking for awhile, they realized that they'd followed a wild animal trail—not their own tracks. They tried to go back to their starting point—but the trailhead never appeared.

Stuart felt himself begin to sweat—and not because of the sun overhead. Hadn't people gotten lost in the woods this way—and died? Why hadn't he used common sense and waited on the trail? He didn't know enough about the wilderness to know which way to go. And from the looks of his buddies, neither did they. Did the group have enough water with them? How cold would they get at night without tents and sleeping bags? Was he really going to die out here in the mountains?

After about thirty minutes, Rick—one of the group's leaders—gave a heavy sigh.

"I guess we're really lost, guys," he admitted, shaking his head.

Stuart's stomach began creeping up his throat.

"I wanted us to get out of here on our own," Rick continued. He reached into his pocket and pulled out something small and round. "But I guess we're going to have to use the compass. The trail should be due north of here."

Compass? Stuart felt his insides untangle themselves. *I guess we're not going to die out here after all!*

When we're lost in the woods, we need a compass to help us find our way. A compass is designed so that no matter where it's located, the needle always points toward the North Pole:

the compass' "true north." Why does this work? How come we can count on a compass to get us out of a tight spot? Because we can depend on the North Pole not to move. It's constant, never changing. We can rely on it to help us find our way.

We need a compass in our spiritual lives as well. Luckily, we've got one—in God. He's dependable, just like the North Pole (but even more so; after all, he's God, who *made* the North Pole). He never changes. We can count on him. Our hearts are the compass needles that point to him. When we're wondering where to go, what to do, our hearts direct us to "true north," and God faithfully points the way.

In the midst of all the voices that tear us down, we desperately need a voice of peace, hope, and strength. And we find it in Jesus. He says:

Are you tired? Worn out? Burned out on religion? Come to me. Get away with me and you'll recover your life. I'll show you how to take real rest. Walk with me and work with me—watch how I do it. Learn the unforced rhythms of grace. I won't lay anything heavy or ill-fitting on you. Keep company with me and you'll learn to live freely and lightly.

MATTHEW 11:28-30, THE MESSAGE

In these words, we find our "true north." When we follow Jesus—when we listen to his voice—he leads us to *real* life. When a compass is broken, its needle swings wildly, all over the place; when *we're* damaged by the voices that harm us, we do the same thing. But when we make God our true north, we stop spinning out of control. We lock on to the good, solid words that come from him. He is the safe place you've been craving! This loving, full-of-acceptance voice drowns out the horrible, lying voices and begins to build us back up again.

The One Voice That Counts

We've already talked about the voices in your world. You know that some of them are good for you, and some are bad. You know how they make you feel *right now*. But can they really impact your tomorrow?

You'd better believe it. In fact, the positive voices are important to your life. In a way, positive voices fuel you up for the road ahead. But the voices that tear you down can drain your tank.

Your body needs fuel, or energy, to keep going. Well, your spirit needs fuel, too. And the "gas" that gives you energy, keeps you going, and lets you do all the things you were put on this earth to do—comes from God. Your main source of this fuel is God's loving messages to you.

That's right: God's messages to *you*. Not just to everyone on earth—though God really does love us all. But he's got tons of things he wants to say to *you*, personally. And it's not just because, as God—the ultimate good guy—he has to. No way! God wants to say good and loving things to you because he's crazy about you. You're worth way more to him than you can possibly imagine.

But I've done bad things, you say. Well, guess what? We all have. That doesn't stop God from loving us. For *sure,* it hasn't stopped him from loving you. Don't believe me? One reason is, you're probably low on fuel. You're not hearing what God has to say to you anymore. Maybe you've never heard his voice in the first place. That's okay. It doesn't mean he hasn't been saying anything to you. It often takes awhile to learn how to hear his voice.

Remember, God's messages to you are very personal. They're encouraging. And they'll never stop coming! God speaks to you because *you need to hear what he has to say to make it—and to enjoy life.* That's why Jesus says: "It takes more than bread to stay alive. It takes a steady stream of words from God's mouth" (Matthew 4:4, THE MESSAGE). When we really connect with God, that's when we really start to live!

Right now, you may be wondering: *That sounds good, but God hasn't passed me any notes lately.* Probably not. But there are lots of ways that God speaks to you, and lots of ways you can connect with him: through prayer, worship, Bible reading and study, listening to good sermons, music, learning from other Christians, experiencing the natural beauty of the world you're in, exploring silence and solitude, journaling, personal retreats, and other activities like that. God is a communicator. He wants to connect—with *you.* He doesn't want you to be beaten down by voices that hurt you. He created you with love, and he wants others to treat you with dignity.

No matter how loud the "bad" voices get, God is speaking over them the good news of his love for you. How much does he love you? Enough to take all the blame for every sinful thing you've thought or done. Enough to take the rap when he was totally innocent so you could go free. That's how badly he wants your total good.

Remember, in this section of *Stressbusters* we're talking about how to increase your resources. There's no better place to start than here, because the biggest resource you have right now—and the greatest resource you will ever have—is your relationship with God. Are you worried because you think your relationship with God is too weak? No worries. It can be strengthened. All you have to do is to want to be close with him. Your weakest connection to God will always help you more than the strongest resource or skill you have apart from him.

STRESSBUSTER:

You've probably heard that it's good to have a "quiet time" with God. But maybe you've thought to yourself: *There's plenty of time to learn how to do that later. I don't know how to read the Bible—it doesn't make sense to me. I don't have the time.* Or: *I don't see how it's going to help me right now—maybe I'll do it when I'm older.*

Reading the Bible may seem like just one more thing to do in the midst of an already packed schedule. You may even see it as a negative stressor. But it's actually a good thing—one that will challenge you and help you to grow. And on a practical level, reading the Bible actually can help *relieve* some of your bad stress. That's because God's Word is filled with encouragement for you, and truths that will help make your life easier. Spending time just sitting and talking with him is actually pretty soothing, too.

Take an hour this week to spend some time with God.

Try reading through one book in the Bible. (Pick a short one, like Galatians, Ephesians, Philippians, Colossians, 1 Peter, 2 Peter, or 1 John.) Spend ten minutes each day, just reading it through (try reading it more than once, over a period of several days) and talking with God about what you read. Spend some quiet time with him, too, just thinking about what you've learned, and seeing what God reveals to your heart during your time together.

STRESSBUSTER:

Look up John 3:16 in your Bible: "For God so loved the world, that he gave his only begotten Son, that whosoever believeth in him should not perish, but have everlasting life." (That's the King James version. Any translation will work.) Now, rewrite it as a message to *you* (which it is), replacing "the world" with *your* name. "For God so loved [your name], that he gave his only begotten Son ..." When you're done, think about this for a minute. How does it make you feel that God did this for you? How much do you think he cares about you? How much would you like him to care? If he cared for you that way, how would that impact your stress level? Picture in your mind that he loves you that much. Now, open your eyes and realize ... he does!

Pick another verse, or several verses, out of the Bible. Just flip through the New Testament until you find one you like. Try this again, substituting your name wherever possible. Try personalizing the Bible this way when you're reading it. It's not cheating! After all, the whole Bible really is a love letter to you!

The world is full of harassing voices that startle us, undermine us, and stomp on our self-concept. We desperately need a central voice that counters all the others: one that lets us know we're loved and that no matter what happens, God is in control. Thankfully, we have that voice. It is God's voice.

It is whispering to you, "I love you," even now. You can't hear it with your ears. But you can read it in God's Word. You can feel it in your spirit. And you can trust it in your heart.

TWO

Connecting With Others

Anna and Lucy became best friends in the fourth grade, and it seemed like they'd stay that way forever. During days on the elementary school playground, they planned their future lives: they'd grow up, marry brothers, live next door to each other, and be friends forever.

But once they started high school, things began to change. Anna became interested in hanging out with the "in" crowd—without Lucy.

"I think it's important for us to have other friends, too," she said. It made sense ... in a way. But Lucy felt betrayed—and left behind.

Soon, Anna began to share a locker with a girl from the popular crowd. And Lucy realized that she was alone in a way she hadn't been in years.

"God," she prayed while she was crying in bed one night. "You know how lonely I am. Could you please send me a new best friend? I need someone to talk to!"

Lucy couldn't imagine where this "new best friend" could come from, unless a new girl moved into the area. But a couple months later, she auditioned for the school play and got a small part. At rehearsals, Lucy started talking with a sophomore she'd never met before. It turned out that this girl was beginning to grow apart from her best friend as well. The two decided to get together to practice lines for the play. It turned out that they had a lot in common. The new girl was even a Christian. Before long, they were hanging out regularly—and were soon inseparable.

God is no dummy. Yeah, he wants you to talk to him about what's going on in your life. Connecting with him is one of the main things you were put on this earth to do. As we've already said, it's the most important resource you have at your disposal. At the same time, he knows that sometimes you need to talk to someone with skin on: a real, live, trusted human being. Why? Because he made us to be close and to love each other.

GOD ON STRESS:
"It is not good for the man to be alone," God said in Genesis 2:18 (NIV). God made this big announcement just before creating a wife for Adam. But the idea doesn't just apply to marriage. It says something very basic about what it means to be human.

To be human is to be in relationships—relationships with friends, parents, brothers and sisters, other students, people we work with, teachers, ... even coaches. We can't *not* be in relationships. It's what we were made to do. A completely non-relational person (if there were such a thing—and there's not) wouldn't be quite human. I mean, that person wouldn't be all he or she was designed to be. We're just not meant to be disconnected from each other.

Of course, we all get lonely at times. That's part of life. You may have figured out by now that the high school and junior high years can be some of the loneliest times of all. You're not alone if you feel that way. (You're actually in the majority.) But we're not meant to be lonely *all the time*. There's just something about closeness that pumps us up and feeds our souls.

Love, Love, Love

Since God made us to be in relationships, he tells us in the Bible about the one thing we need to be really close with others—and that's love. But he's talking about a very specific *kind* of love.

STRESS 101:

Actually, there are lots of different types of love. In the English language, we have just one word for love. But in the Greek language, there are many names for it. Since several books of the Bible were originally written in Greek, we can see exactly what kind of love God's talking about.

For example, in the Greek, the New Testament talks about *philios* (FEE-lee-ohs) love: an emotional, conditional kind of love that depends on what we get out of a relationship. This is a love that asks, "What's in it for me?" There's also *eros* (AIR-ohs): the Greek word for physical, sexual love. But the love God emphasizes in the Bible is the greatest kind of love: *agape* (uh-GAH-pay). This is a love that's all about bringing good to others, even if it costs us something ourselves. (Picture Jesus on the cross.)

The more *agape* there is, the safer the relationship.

The opposite of *agape* is something that calls itself "love," but is really just the control or manipulation of others. (You've seen this in people who've pressured someone to sleep with them, or to lie or cheat for them.) Because our world often calls this "love," it's easy to get sucked into these kinds of relationships. After all, we all want to be loved. But this kind of "love" makes relationships totally unsafe. If you haven't been hurt by this kind of "love" before, you probably are close to someone who has, or you'll likely be faced with it in some form, someday. And this kind of love hurts—*badly.*

When "Love" Makes Unreasonable Demands

Angel has been best friends with Ginny since their sophomore year of high school. Now, as seniors, they're almost adults. But Ginny's future doesn't look so bright to Angel, because Ginny started taking drugs six months ago. More recently, she's even started dealing.

Angel confronted her for the first time when Ginny started using.

"I love you, Gin," she said sadly. "You're my best friend."

"Yeah? Well, if you love me," Ginny insisted, "you won't judge me."

Not wanting to make her friend angry, Angel backed off. But now, she's beginning to feel even more uncomfortable. She's worried that Ginny's hurting herself—and the people who are buying drugs from her. Angel is even beginning to get pulled into Ginny's mess; several times, Ginny has lied to her parents, telling them that she was going over to Angel's house, when she was really meeting a customer or friends who use. It's only a matter of time before Angel herself is forced to either lie for Ginny or give her away. She doesn't want to cover up for her friend but neither does she want to lose her.

Worst of all, Ginny has offered drugs to Angel a couple of times—and Angel has thought about taking them, just once, to save the friendship.

If This Is Love, Why Am I So Miserable?

How can you protect yourself from this kind of so-called "love" and others like it? By connecting only with people who are safe. I'm not saying that you should only love people who are safe. We're supposed to love all the people God made. "Love others as well as you love yourself" (Mark 12:31, THE MESSAGE).

But there's a difference between loving people and connecting with them. When we connect with people, we go deeper than casual, everyday conversations. We let those people into our hearts and souls. You only want to do that with safe people.

What are some characteristics of safe people? Safe people are trustworthy. They don't give double messages. They see and care not only about what they want, but what you need. They respect your personal space. They do what they say they'll do—and if they don't, they apologize and don't make excuses. Let's look at an example. Here's a conversation between two guys, Jack and Arnie, who were supposed to get together to hang out. One's safe; the other, unsafe.

JACK: Hey, where were you yesterday, Arn? I waited for you for, like, half an hour. You said you'd be at the bike shop at four.

ARNIE: Yeah, I know. My dad called just before I left the house and said I had to mow the yard.

JACK: Bummer. Why didn't you call me last night? I wondered what was up.

ARNIE (casually): Oh ... you know. I figured you'd already left.

JACK (starting to get upset): You could at least have left a message at my house, telling me what happened.

ARNIE: Yeah, well ... I guess I didn't think about it.

JACK: This is the third time you've done this in the last month! Didn't you tell your dad I was waiting for you?

ARNIE: (mumbles something)

JACK: What?

ARNIE (sheepishly): Um ... He wouldn't let me use the phone. He said I should have thought of that the day before.

JACK: *The day before?* Wait a minute. You mean, you already knew you were going to have to mow? He'd already asked you to? And you told me your dad called "just before" you left? You wanted me to think he sprang it on you at the last minute! Look, man, if you want to be friends, you're going to have to stop lying to me.

How do you think Jack feels when he finds out Arnie hasn't been completely honest with him? What does Jack do to make sure Arnie doesn't treat him this way anymore? Does he overreact?

Should he put up with lying just because he's not supposed to "judge others"?

Actually, what Jack does is pretty healthy. He refuses to let himself get confused or beaten down by his friend's actions. He puts up healthy boundaries, telling Arnie he's not going to put up with being treated poorly. Yeah, it's important to Jack to have friends. But he also knows enough to blow off the idea that he should "be nice" and "save" the relationship no matter what it costs him.

Any relationship that keeps you hurting or turning yourself into a pretzel to make someone else happy isn't really a relationship. It's just sort of an "arrangement." It's hanging out together, but without real friendship.

Jack knows that if he ignores or excuses Arnie's untruthfulness, he'll just be encouraging his friend to keep acting that way. That wouldn't be good for Arnie, or for anyone who will ever be in his life. Ignoring Arnie's flakiness would make the relationship unsafe. It would allow one person (Arnie) to use another person (Jack) as a doormat. God never takes our wellbeing lightly. He never treats us like doormats, and he doesn't want us to treat each other that way, either.

Getting Safe

If we're going to connect safely with others, we need to do three things:

1. recognize safe people,[1]

2. become safe people ourselves, and
3. speak up when someone is manipulative or possessive, or treats us badly in any other way.

Once we do these things, we make it possible for ourselves to open up and become vulnerable about what's bothering us in life. We solve the loneliness problem by connecting, but only with reasonably safe people. (I say "reasonably safe" because no one's perfect, and anyone can inadvertently hurt or confuse us. It's important to give feedback to these safe people, too.)

Unfortunately, many teens solve the loneliness problem by accepting *any* form of connection.

Sandra felt that all the kids in her high school youth group had more money than she did. She was embarrassed that her clothes, jewelry, and home didn't measure up to theirs, so she stopped hanging out with them.

After that, she was lonely but didn't know how to tell anyone. So it felt strange but good when an older boy sidled up to her at school and said, "Hey, Sandra. You're looking *good* today." Sandra knew this guy's reputation wasn't the greatest, but she thought maybe he'd gotten a bad rap.

At first, Sandra was a little nervous. Yeah, she wanted the attention. Still, she chose to believe in the best in him. And she made sure he knew exactly where she stood in her faith and values. In fact, on their second date, she informed him that she was going to remain a virgin until her wedding night. When she said this, Eddie smiled and squeezed her hand, and told her that he loved that about her. Sandra figured, *At least he appreciates my values and is going to respect them.*

About a month later, though, Eddie began to push Sandra physically. Sandra knew what he was doing was wrong, and she told him it made her uncomfortable. But by this time, she was hooked; she was so attached to Eddie, she couldn't imagine breaking up with him. So she tried instead to make him happy while maintaining her values as much as she could.

Before long, Eddie began to touch her in places she'd told him not to. At first, she tried to push his hands away. But it seemed easier to let him have his way, at least a little bit. As long as she kept her virginity, Sandra reasoned, she was okay.

But one night things went too far. Sandra told Eddie no, but he kept going and she didn't know how to stop it. After that, she didn't have her virginity to protect anymore. In tears, she told Eddie it couldn't happen again. But this time, he told her she'd have to keep sleeping with him—or he'd find someone else who would.

"You don't understand," he said condescendingly. "It's too hard for a guy to stop. It *hurts*. If you loved me, you'd just do it."

Sandra has decided to go along with what Eddie wants. She doesn't feel like she has any other choice. She needs to keep Eddie now. She's lost her virginity, and she's sure no "good" guy will want her anymore. In her mind, Eddie is all she has left.

Sandra has exchanged one source of stress (loneliness) for a whole boatload of new stressors (sexual pressure, a nagging conscience, lying to her parents, fear of pregnancy, fear of sexually transmitted disease, loss of self-respect, etc.). She's not the only one. Lots of teens unexpectedly add to their stress by making bad choices while trying to deal with the pain in their lives. This is just one more reason why it's so important to find trustworthy people you can open up with.

Sadly, the irresponsible choices we make often make the negative voices inside us even worse. You could say, "Bad choices lead to bad voices." Because of the poor decisions she made, Sandra is beginning to say to herself, *Everyone knows what you are. You might as well keep doing what you're doing, because no one's ever going to think you're good and clean again. You're dirty. No good guy, or good friend, is ever going to want you now.* The lying voices are louder than ever.

Because bad choices lead to bad relationships, it is *really* important to know the difference between who's safe and who's not. If we refuse to learn how to tell who's safe, then we become an unsafe person to ourselves.

STRESSBUSTER:

Are you in any relationship that feels unsafe? A friend-ship? A romantic relationship? A family relationship? What, exactly, is unsafe about this person? What's safe about him or her—anything?

Make a list of things you can do to make the relation-ship safer. What are some boundaries you can set—some rules that you both have to live by? Have you talked to this person about how you feel? Do you even *know* how you feel, exactly? Make a list of the emotions you experience in this relationship. Are you angry? Afraid? Confused? Lonely? Hurt? Take some time to journal about these things. Then set a time to talk with this person, or a safe adult, about your feelings.

If there's nothing you can do to make the relationship safer, it may be time to end it. (Obviously, you can't do this if it's a sibling, or someone else you're in a permanent relationship with.) Spend some time talking with God about this. Ask him to guide you. Listen to what your heart tells you within the confines of prayer. Talk to your mom or dad, a trusted pastor, youth leader, or school counselor. Pray for wisdom and strength, and for new friends to fill the gap. Try to end the relationship in a way that honors the other person and shows him or her respect—and God's love.

STRESSBUSTER:

For one more look at who's safe and who's not, read the following columns. Then think about the people you're close to. How do they measure up? Are there other people you need to pull away from a little bit? Are you willing to put up with some loneliness for a little while in order to make room in your life for safe people who love you really well?

Connect with people who:
- do what they say they'll do
- are honest
- can think about you, not just themselves
- pay close attention to needs you express

Don't connect with people who:
- give you double messages
- leave you consistently confused*
- are controlling
- are manipulative
- only talk about themselves
- never apologize

The truth is, we are not made to live in isolation. Everything in us is geared toward closeness with people who are safe. These kinds of supportive, honest relationships serve as some of the biggest stressbusters in our lives.

Don't forget that you need to be a safe person, too. Don't stress out about this! Just think about ways you can improve in this area and resolve to make those changes.

*For more help on confusion and its role in deciding who's safe and who's unsafe, read chapter seven in Part II of this book: "Dealing With Confusing Adults."

THREE

Getting Real

Last night, fifteen-year-old Sam's dad committed an unpardonable sin: he cut Sam's hair. Ever since Sam turned thirteen, he has pleaded to be allowed to go to a haircutting pro. But his dad insists, "Every home haircut is fifteen bucks in the bank."

It's true that Sam's family saved some money. But today, Sam is at school with true "dreadlocks"—the kind of hair you simply dread to be seen with. Talk about stress!

By the time Sam gets home, his feelings are at flood stage. He knows he feels anger. But other emotions are simmering under the surface: humiliation, helplessness, hatred, despair, foolishness, self-hatred, emptiness, and sadness. Sam is aware of only a fraction of these emotions.

This isn't really his fault. He has been trained by his parents his entire life to keep most "bad" emotions under wraps. Just like Sam, his dad and mom freely express anger, but bury other challenging emotions. Sam's experience with TV and movies also has provided him with negative role models who constantly vent their anger, often through violence. Arnold P. Goldstein and Ellen McGinnis explain in *Skillstreaming the Adolescent,* "There are an average of 6 violent acts per hour on prime-time evening programming and 25 such acts per hour on Saturday morning cartoons. By age 16, youngsters have seen 200,000 violent acts, about 30,000 of them murders or attempted murders."[1] The video games Sam plays also invite him to engage in angry, violent actions, such as killing everyone on the screen (and the next screen, and the next).

Sam is so used to anger, in fact, it's become second nature for him to direct *all* his feelings into anger. Anger makes him feel (at least momentarily) big, not small. It allows him to feel competent, not stupid. Anger covers up painful feelings like sadness or helplessness.

It also has a high action component. Anger "wants" to do something, so Sam is ready to *do* something, too. This is why he clobbers his little brother over nothing after he gets home, and why when Sam's mom asks him to set the table he goes to his room instead, provoking—you guessed it—her anger.

Is there an alternative for Sam and his family? You bet. But if they are going to get real and eliminate the tremendous stress this situation adds to their lives, they need to learn how to recognize and express all their feelings—not just anger. They need to create a "feelings vocabulary."

STRESS 101:

Did you know that how you handle stress affects how long you live? It's true. If you're like most teenagers, you're not worried right now about what your life will look like when you're eighty years old or fifty ... or even thirty. But those days will come sooner than you expect! And the decisions you make *now* will affect your quality of life *then*.

Experts agree that stress can make you more vulnerable to disease. At the same time, coping with stress in healthy ways can make you *less* vulnerable. The question is, do you care? Will you just live for today, not worrying about what happens tomorrow? Or will you make a conscious choice *right now* to establish patterns that can improve the quality and length of your life?

If You Can't Name It, You Can't Claim It

Two months ago, Neil told his best friend Chris about a crush he has on Karly, a cute girl he's had his eye on all year. Since then, Neil has been trying to work up the courage to ask Karly out.

Finally, last week, he got up his nerve. Casually, he dropped down beside Karly in the lunchroom as she ate her pizza.

"Hey, Karly," he said, trying to sound cool and composed. "What's up? Watcha doin' this weekend?"

"Oh, didn't Chris tell you?" Karly looked vaguely surprised. Chris and Neil told each other everything. "He's taking me to the batting cages Friday night, and then we're going to catch a movie."

Neil was stunned. Later that afternoon, Chris came into Biology and slapped him on the back. Neil gave him a short nod. "Hey, bud." Chris narrowed his eyes at him, looking suspicious. "What's up?"

Neil pushed back the feelings that were rising in him. "Nothing." He shrugged. "I'm just beat. My dad had me clean out the garage all yesterday afternoon." Chris looked at him, then nodded and turned away.

Neil had a perfect opportunity to let his feelings help him. He could have told Chris how much his betrayal had hurt him.

Neil could have stood up for himself. He could have established healthy boundaries in friendship, letting Chris know that he expected him to respect his feelings by at least *warning* him if he was going to ask out a girl Neil liked. But facing the pain was too hard, or so he thought. It was easier to pretend that nothing was wrong.

God gave us a wide range of emotions, and for good reason. Our emotions are there to help us, to protect us, to teach us and, yes, to relieve our stress. Each is a key to a better, healthier life. But if we don't recognize and acknowledge our emotions, we can't benefit from them. Worse, the feelings we don't acknowledge always rise to the surface in some other way, just as Sam's feelings of hurt and frustration came out in his anger toward his little brother.

Often, the reason we don't recognize our feelings is that we're not used to acknowledging and talking about them. That's why we, like Neil and like Sam's family, need a "feelings vocabulary." Having a "feelings vocabulary" means that we can express "negative" emotions like weakness and sadness when that's what we really feel.

Why should we? Because it opens a door to our hearts that would otherwise remain closed. Feelings that go unnamed soon turn silent and go AWOL (Absent Without Leave). They're not really gone; they're just lurking, waiting to show up in some other form.

It's easy to replace these misplaced emotions with whatever feelings we *are* willing to admit—maybe anger or a forced happiness or a vaguely sad mood—none of which lessen our stress or help us grow. When we rely on a couple of stock emotional responses, we feel dead. It becomes harder than ever to hear what God is saying to us—a big problem in light of our desire to lessen our stress, since God is, as we have already said, our greatest resource to living a low-stress life.

One day in Civics class, Carrie's teacher led his students in a spirited debate about capital punishment. As the discussion progressed, it became clear that most of Carrie's classmates believed in the death penalty. Carrie did not, and she quietly but firmly expressed her views.

The teacher, a supporter of the death penalty, challenged her publicly, pushing Carrie hard to defend her position. Because Carrie is very shy, she clammed up and remained embarrassed for the rest of the class over her inability to talk about her convictions.

After class, Carrie felt vaguely unhappy. She tried to push the incident out of her mind, but the feelings wouldn't go away. That night, she sat on her bed, thinking about what had happened that day. In her journal, she wrote, "Mr. Heath makes me so mad! How could he do that to me? I was so humiliated! It's a teacher's job to teach, but what he did was *bully* me." As Carrie continued to write, she began to get in touch with other, less obvious emotions.

Later, before bed, Carrie's mom came into her room and asked her about her mood. Carrie shared with her mom some of what she was feeling: embarrassment, anger, and betrayal. Her mom listened quietly and finally asked: "What do you want to do about it?"

Carrie considered, then said, "I don't know. I guess I want to tell Mr. Heath how he made me feel."

"I think that's a good idea," her mom agreed. That night, Carrie prayed for strength to do just that.

The next day, Carrie went to Mr. Heath before class and told him how she was feeling. She didn't get a public apology, but Mr. Heath did tell her that he was sorry he had made her feel uncomfortable. More importantly, Carrie learned that she could stand up for herself, and that her feelings and opinions are worth defending.

GOD ON STRESS:

Stressed out about a friendship, a class, or some other problem at school? Worried about your dad's job or your aunt's illness? Take it to God in prayer. He's the one who's in charge. He'll hear you. He cares for you. Stress generally comes when we can't control our situations. But God is *always* in control. He says, "Come to me, all you who are weary and burdened, and I will give you rest. Take my yoke upon you and learn from me, for I am gentle and humble in heart, and you will find rest for your souls. For my yoke is easy and my burden is light" (Matthew 11:28-30, NIV).

Our Emotions Know the Real Story

Carrie felt upset, angry, hurt. None of these emotions are very fun. But they're all perfectly acceptable, both in this world **and** in the eyes of God. In fact, the Bible is all about dialing into your honest feelings.

In Psalm 62 (NIV), for example, the psalmist, David, says things like, "My soul finds rest in God alone" (David desperately wants peace), "[God] is my fortress, I will never be shaken" (he needs encouragement), "My hope comes from [God]" (he longs for hope), "Pour out your hearts to him, for God is our refuge" (David needs God and knows he cannot make it on his own), "You, O God, are strong" (God makes him feel secure when he doesn't feel secure on his own). In reading verses like these, we see that, whatever his faults, David was alive at heart. We recognize the courage he and other psalmists demonstrated by opening up to the God who rules the universe, even when their emotions were hard ones.

Unfortunately, not very many of us feel at home with our emotions. They hit us hard, stay too long, and leave us drained, like relatives who overstay their welcome. But why aren't we more okay with our feelings?

Some experts suggest that our emotions were originally intended to motivate us toward flight or fight. When a caveman felt fear, he knew to turn and run or else attack. *Our* emotions don't usually involve life-or-death consequences.

Still, some scientists stick to evolutionary theory. Many suggest that love is nothing but a string of chemical reactions in our brains. Instead of "I love you," we should say, "My brain chemistry exhibits certain configurations in response to stimuli from you" (try saying *that* on a date, and see where it gets you!). Unfortunately, when we hear this kind of thing, our hearts lose touch with the story God is telling. We wonder, *How can God be telling a good story about me, if that "me" is only a purposeless batch of sophisticated neuronal wiring?*

The more we lose touch with God's great, amazing, happy-ending story, the less our hearts have a story big enough to help us thrive. The human heart needs a *big* story. No wonder we're uncomfortable with our emotions: They're often telling us that our stories are too small.

Here's what I mean. Say your boyfriend or girlfriend breaks up with you. You're devastated, especially when you find out that he or she has been seeing someone else on the sly for a month. You're mad, hurt, despairing. Three days after your breakup, a close friend says, "Get over it. Move on. You're overreacting. It's not worth it." If you listen, you'll be tempted to stuff all those healthy feelings, maybe even to move on quickly to someone else. (How many times have you seen your friends start up new relationships too soon, just because they were trying to put a lid on feelings of sadness, depression, or loneliness?)

It would be better to blow off your friend's well-meaning advice. Here's a better approach: Don't get over your emotions, get into them! Don't wallow in them, but acknowledge them. Talk about them with people you trust. You may just discover that your heart is telling you you're made for a story where people don't lie, aren't two-faced, keep commitments, and are careful with your heart.

You are made for a story where your dreams are taken seriously—so seriously that people (both Jesus and others in your life who love you) willingly make enormous sacrifices to help make your dreams a reality. You're made for a happy ending, laughter, kindness, challenge, adventure, and hope. When this isn't what your life looks like, your "negative" emotions are there to remind you of what you're really made for.

But How Do I Get There?

Carrie learned a lot about what she was feeling by journaling and talking with her mom. But when she needed to find the strength to talk about her hard emotions, she turned to God.

What is the one way you and I can bring together our selves and our emotions? Through honest prayer and worship.

Talk to God in Truth

Honest prayer is where we ask God for the strength and hope to step into the story he has for us, even when it feels bad for awhile. Honesty is crucial to prayer because sometimes we need to tell God about what it's costing us to live in a world that's *not* telling God's story.

Have you been encouraged to be honest with God—or do you think you're only supposed to talk with him about what you *like* in your life? Do you know the joy of talking to him without having to sound completely "together"? Without having to sound religious? Without having to always sound cheerful? God doesn't require any of that from you. He wants you to talk to him right where you are, just as you are.

When we use our feelings vocabulary in prayer, we get better at telling God what's going on inside us. In the Psalms this is called "pouring out your heart." Psalm 62:8 (NASB) says, "Trust in him at all times, O people; Pour out your heart before him. God is a refuge for us." Honest prayer is taking your heart, like a cup, and emptying it all out before God. Pouring out your heart means hiding nothing, pretending about nothing. It's prayer without a "delete" button. God can't fill a cup that's already full. You must pour it all out—fear, confusion, discouragement, boredom, heartbreak—so he can begin to refill you. Only when you tell God everything can he be everything you need. He will nourish, encourage, guide, correct, befriend, and love you.

GOD ON STRESS:

"The Lord is a refuge for the oppressed, a stronghold in times of trouble. Those who know your name will trust in you, for you, Lord, have never forsaken those who seek you" (Psalm 9:9, NIV).

Adoring Him in Love

Along with honest prayer comes worship. Worship is when your thankful spirit teams up with a heart that is blown away by all that God has done for you. What happens when we mingle awe and gratefulness? We learn two things: One, that we're *not* the center of the universe (thank goodness) and, two, we don't have to be in control (breathe another sigh of relief).

I don't know about you, but I'm tired of trying to be the center of everything. I get sick of wondering, "How am I doing?" "How am I looking?" "Do they think I'm a loser?" This kind of thinking makes us anxious. It makes us measure ourselves against others. It turns others into competitors instead of people who might care about us, and who we might care about. It makes us try to control life instead of enjoying it. In other words, it stresses us out.

Freedom from being at the center allows us to experiment,

take risks (and possibly look ridiculous), clown around, and have fun! When we are fighting to remain at the center, we have to worry about image, not dropping the ball, looking stupid, managing others, meeting expectations, and squashing our talents and gifts (because they might threaten others). No wonder we're worn out!

When we are struck by the awesomeness of God, we are able to get ourselves off-center, so God can be at the center. We lose our obsession with control, because he's in control, and we lose our fear of our emotions, because God is bigger than anything our feelings might be telling us.

God is awesome and sovereign, but he's also close and comforting. He wants us on his lap. He's the King of kindness who says, "Come to me if you're tired and overloaded, and I'll give you rest" (paraphrase of Matthew 11:28). In his restful presence, we can get real with our emotions and draw from his strength as we talk them over with him.

Honest prayer and worship lead us to someone whose big heart can receive our feelings and put them into perspective. This is the path to true refuge from out-of-control stress. This is the way we embrace our emotions, get real with ourselves, and become the whole people God wants us to be.

FOUR

Doing the Truth

Stacey, Bill, and Kevin grew up in the same neighborhood and have been friends for years. Since their freshman year, the three have been practically inseparable, and all are involved in a local church youth group.

Stacey loves Bill like a brother, but she knows he can be a bit pushy, even obnoxious at times. One weekend while Kevin is out of town, the youth group gathers to watch movies until midnight. In between two of the films, Bill starts teasing about one of the movies the girls in the group picked out, calling it a "chick flick" and making faces.

"Honestly, Bill," complains Jill, a friend of Stacey's, "if you don't like the movie, then leave. No one's stopping you."

While the girls nod their agreement and the guys jeer, Bill turns to Stacey for support. She shrugs and whispers, "I'm sorry," but he is already storming off. She feels bad for Bill, but she also knows he brought the whole thing on himself.

The next Monday at school, Stacey is talking to Kevin about his weekend when Bill approaches, looking like he's swallowed a hornet's nest.

"Thanks a lot for *not* backing me up Friday night," Bill snaps. Stacey tries to explain, but he cuts her off and stomps away, leaving Stacey almost in tears.

Later, Kevin takes Bill aside in the hall and says, "You kind of leveled Stacey awhile ago, don't you think? Wasn't that a bit harsh?" Bill looks surprised.

Bill had walked off so fast, he didn't even see the tears in Stacey's eyes—though he should have seen the hurt in them. He won't even be aware that, during the next week at school, Stacey will be avoiding him. It's not that he doesn't care, he just doesn't notice.

Why? Bill doesn't see Stacey's unhappiness because he doesn't *want* to. Seeing often brings pain to the person doing the seeing.

Like Bill, you and I can overlook reality when it makes us uncomfortable or makes us unhappy. But just as we need to get real with our feelings, it's important for us to recognize the truth of our lives so we can respond appropriately. When we don't do this, stress is a huge result.

Of course, it's much easier to remain blind. But choosing *not* to see doesn't solve our problems for long—if at all. Not seeing throws us into a world of lies and self-deception. And this way of living is *really* stressful.

Let's say a group of girls share with their guy friends in the ski club that they feel uncomfortable around their adult club advisor. They report that he stands too close, puts his arm around them a lot, looks them over from head to toe, and comments a bit too appreciatively about what they're wearing. But the guys in the group say, "No way. You're just overreacting. He's a good guy, and you're not going to ruin the ski club for us." The girls are really hurt and a little scared. They don't know what to do next.

If the girls are right about their advisor, the guys have chosen denial and self-interest over their friends' well-being. The guys also have put the girls down, depicting them as being overly sensitive. Now the guys have two big problems: strained friendships and bad consciences. Because they need to lie to themselves to keep their consciences quiet, they make excuses like, "Girls see problems everywhere. They're just weird. Why can't they chill out like us?" Now the guys have strained friendships, painful consciences, *and* hearts loaded with self-deception.

By choosing not to see, they've just added a bunch of new problems to the original dilemma, which is not going away. The result? The core group within the ski club begins to come apart, bringing the guys and the girls both major stress.

STRESS 101:

What is stress? According to Brockhampton References' *Understanding Stress*, stress is: "the 'wear and tear' our minds and bodies experience when we attempt to cope with our continually changing environment."*

Think about all the changes in your life over the last few years: making new friends and separating from old ones, starting a new school, getting new teachers, learning to drive, relating to your parents as a teenager rather than as a child. If you feel stressed out, be assured that this is *normal*. After all, who could experience a more "continually changing environment" than a teen?

* *Understanding Stress* (London: Brockhampton, 1996), 9.

To See or Not to See: That Is the Question

So if seeing brings pain and stress, and *not* seeing also brings pain and stress, what do we do? It depends on what kind of pain/stress combination we want to feel. Seeing usually brings constructive pain, and with it good stress that causes us to grow, while not seeing brings destructive pain and bad, damaging stress.

What is the difference? Constructive pain and stress help you face reality, decide whether to confront someone, take responsibility, learn to make a difference, be competent as a person, be a truth-teller to yourself and others, solidify relationships worth keeping, and let those go that are not. Destructive pain and stress cause you to avoid reality, dodge confrontation, act irresponsibly, feel you can't make a difference, live ineffectively and in self-deception, and tolerate unhealthy relationships.

Here's an example of someone who has a choice between these two options. Mary wanted to go to the prom, but no one had asked her yet. So she asked her friend Jack, who goes to a different high school, to go with her. Jack agreed. Because Mary knows that Jack stays very busy, she asked him to double-check his schedule for possible conflicts. He reported back, "A-okay. I'm free to go."

Two weeks before the prom, Jack calls Mary and says, "I didn't tell you I was auditioning for a play because I didn't think I'd get the part, but I *did* get it." It turns out that prom night is also dress rehearsal night for the play. Jack's plan is that he'll leave as soon as play practice is over, change into his tux, pick up Mary, and get to the prom at about 10:00 P.M.

Mary tells Jack that sounds all right, but she's disappointed. She'll miss the dress-up dinner out with friends she and Jack were going to before the prom. She'll miss half the prom itself.

Mary shares her frustration with her friends. They say Jack is being really selfish. At first, Mary defends him, saying, "This play really means a lot to him." But her friends insist, "Then he should have let you know way ahead of time that he was auditioning—especially when you asked him to check his schedule!"

Mary realizes she's at a fork in the road: she's going to have to either face Jack's selfishness or deny it. If she sees the situation clearly, she'll get pain and stress, but it'll be a constructive pain and stress that will help her decide whether to confront Jack's self-centeredness.

If she refuses to see it, she'll experience the destructive pain and negative stress of having to lie to herself about what's happening. Worse, she may be tempted to attribute Jack's choice to some flaw in herself, thinking: "Nobody else seems to think I'm worth anything, and now Jack has joined the club. I'm just a loser. I guess I'm lucky he wants to go with me at all." Heading down this path will set her up for accepting crumbs from others, possibly for the rest of her life. Mary deserves better.

So do you.

STRESS 101:

Why does stress exist? It's simple. Stress was designed to spur us to action. In the early days of humankind, stress helped people to survive. What happened when a dangerous wild animal approached? Stress! That stress told the person's brain how to direct the body. The body would tense, the heart would race, adrenaline would rush in, and the man or woman would *get out of there or fight!* Stress was a response to an immediate threat (the wild animal). Once it was dealt with, the stress was over. No long-term effects.

Today, things are very different. We don't feel stress about becoming lunch for some carnivorous creature, but about things like college, going on dates, and our relationships with our parents. When we face stress, our bodies tense, our heart rates soar, and adrenaline rushes through our veins (similar to what happened to our ancestors). But there is no immediate showdown for us as there once was with a wild bear. Instead, stress sticks with us. Rather than getting stressed occasionally, we are more often stressed than *not*. We worry not just about things that do happen, but about thousands of things that simply *could* happen. The result? Our bodies and minds suffer long-term effects of stress, and many of us suffer from short-term illnesses, like colds, headaches, and indigestion as well as long-term stress-related disease, such as heart disease and high blood pressure.

Does knowing this stress you out? Good—because that stress can spur you to action! By learning to deal with your stress in healthy ways, you can greatly offset these negative effects of stress. Read on!

Choosing the Truth

Are you ready to choose helpful pain instead of destructive pain? If so, you'll find that this requires you to make a stand much more often. As a result, you'll need God more than ever. Turning to God brings you to someone who suffered constructive pain in giving up his own Son. He knows what to do with that kind of pain and can help you.

As Mary tries to decide how to deal with her problem, she prays, "Lord, show me what to do." Then she remembers a Scripture verse that she heard at a recent Christian concert: "*Speaking the truth in love,* we will in all things grow up into him who is the Head, that is, Christ" (Ephesians 4:15, NIV, italics mine). She prays about this, then gives Jack a call.

"Look," she says, "I realize you're in a bad spot, but I feel really disappointed. I don't think you understand just how much I was looking forward to this, or how awful this makes me feel."

"Really?" Jack thinks about this. "Well, what do you want me to do?" He doesn't really see any way out.

"I'd like you to ask if you can be excused from the dress rehearsal. You aren't playing one of the major leads. I'll bet the director will let you off if you explain. Or maybe he'd be willing to start a couple hours earlier, and let you off early."

"Maybe." Jack considers her proposal. "I guess I can ask. But I can't promise anything."

"I know," Mary tells him. "But I'd like you to try. You owe me that much."

"You're right," Jack agrees after a moment. The weight of the situation is finally beginning to hit him. "Look, I really am sorry about all this." The apology goes a long way toward making Mary feel better.

Because of Mary's call, Jack now has to think about his actions, and Mary is freed up from a lot of bad feelings that could arise from the situation. Confronting Jack was hard, but helped her feel better about herself.

The verse Mary remembered talks about "speaking the truth in love." Actually, the verse could better be translated, "truthing in love" or "doing the truth in love." What it's saying is, not just in our words but in every part of our lives, we grow up by being honest and facing what's true. Jesus talks about the benefits of "truthing" from another angle when he says, "You will know the truth, and the truth will set you free" (John 8:32, NIV). You can be free from lies, deception, manipulation, and other behaviors that come between you and your God. These are major promises from God to you. So how can you take advantage of those promises by starting to "do the truth"? By getting feedback, getting into God's Word, getting ahold of God's grace, and getting an understanding of why we would choose any other path.

Get the Scoop

We do the truth, first, *by opening up to feedback.* By this, I mean both positive and negative feedback.

"Wait," you might say (and I wouldn't blame you), "are you saying anybody can walk right up to me and dump all their opinions on me?" *Absolutely not.* I'm *not* saying you should take as gospel everything anybody and everybody says about you. Ephesians 4:15 talks about speaking (or doing) the truth "in love." In other words, those who aren't acting in love *cannot* dump their version of truth on you or anyone else. Truth in the hands of an unloving person is a firearm. No amount of truth-telling excuses malice or indifference. First Corinthians 13:1-3 puts it this way:

> If I speak with human eloquence and angelic ecstasy but don't love, I'm nothing but the creaking of a rusty gate.
>
> If I speak God's Word with power, revealing all his mysteries and making everything plain as day, and if I have faith that says to a mountain, "Jump," and it jumps, but I don't love, I'm nothing.
>
> If I give everything I own to the poor and even go to the stake to be burned as a martyr, but I don't love, I've gotten nowhere. So, no matter what I say, what I believe, and what I do, I'm bankrupt without love.
>
> 1 CORINTHIANS 13:1-3, THE MESSAGE

Only seek feedback, then, from those you can sense are loving people. Concerning even these people, you should remind yourself, "This input is not straight from God. I need to let it settle in and pray about it to see how much to keep and how much to toss." People can tell us a lot about ourselves, and we should value their insights. But they can also be wrong. They are only human—just like us.

Get a Word From God

Second, we do the truth *by looking into the mirror of God's Word.* Why would we want to do this—I mean really *want* to without being forced by guilt or pressure? For many adolescents (and adults, too) reading the Bible has all the attraction of memorizing the phone book. This is because the Bible is often presented as an information bank instead of as a story that answers our heart's cry: "Will somebody tell me something good that I can trust and lean on?"

While the information in the Bible is important, what is even *more* important is the God who calls to our hearts through all that information. We often treat the Bible as a rule book, rather than as the love letter it really is. That love shows us the *big picture* of who God is and what he's up to in our world.

Stress, on the other hand, is usually about the small picture, or the details. The more stressed we are, the more our perspective shrinks down to a tiny point, where all we want is one thing: "Get me out of this pain, right now!"

How does the big picture help us? By influencing how we face life and its stress. Most of us probably have followed this ineffective sequence when faced with stress: *react* to the stressor, *reduce* (or shrink) our perspective, and *repeat* the same old behavior. But God's Word calls us into a new and different pattern: to *reflect* on the truth, to *realize* that growth comes through "doing the truth," and to *respond* in a positive, healthy manner.

Do you see a situation in your life right now where you need to look into the big picture of God's Word to help you *reflect, realize,* and *respond?* Write these three words across the top of a sheet of paper or in your journal. Dive into God's Word and start jotting down ideas under each word. Here's what Mary might have written in her situation:

reflect
The Lord says that truth will help me grow. The truth might help Jack grow as well. There must be a link between truth and maturing.

realize
The truth is that I'm disappointed in Jack's thoughtlessness. He really should have told me the whole story up front.

respond
I'm going to tell Jack what I need, and I hope it helps him shrink that blind spot of his.

On the other hand, under the *old* sequence Mary might have had the following messages swirling around in her head:

react
If I confront Jack, he'll just put it back on me. It's my fault for asking him. What was I thinking?

reduce perspective
I'm a fool for expecting to be treated well; I want too much, which also makes me look like a fool; I need to get real and admit that life's not going to give me much.

repeat old behaviors
Go with Jack at 10:00 P.M. Tell myself I don't really miss going out with my friends that much; be cool toward Jack all evening just to show him he can't just have anything he wants.

Get a Grip on Grace

Third, we "do the truth" *by relaxing into God's grace.* Grace means if you have trusted in Christ you are no longer on trial. Grace is abundant; it overflows even when—make that *especially* when—you sin. Grace can't be used up. It just keeps coming. There's more than enough of it to go around. That means you can de-stress and relax!

There are many pictures of grace in Scripture: God's kindness toward Cain, God's love toward David, Jesus' kindnesses to the woman at the well and to the woman caught in adultery, the story of a father's love for his prodigal son, Jesus' restoration of Peter, and so much more.

The clearest verse that defines grace may come in the question Paul asks in Romans 8:33 (NIV), "Who will bring any charge against those whom God has chosen?" The answer, of course, is *"No one!"* There is no source in the universe that can justly accuse even one of God's people. The charges against us *have been dropped forever.* There's no greater stressbuster than that!

reflect	realize	respond
God tells me that I'm off the hook with him. Because of Christ, I'm totally forgiven. I'll never be punished by the Lord in this world or the next.	I can now face that faultfinder in my head, the one that never shuts up. I can stop taking the blame for everything that goes wrong.	When the faultfinder's "voice" interrupts me, I'm going to blow it off by reading Romans 8:31-39. And I'm going to find out what I get from listening to that voice (see next page about "payoff").

Remember, grace means you can relax!

Get to the Root

Fourth, we "do the truth" by asking ourselves, *"What's the pay-off self-deception brings me?"* We can unpack this idea by looking over Jessica's shoulder.

Jessica is unhappy in her family. This is not uncommon. A lot of people feel like "black sheep." They feel as though they don't quite fit in, or that they're somehow unacceptable. The truth is, wild, tomboy Jessica is very different from her gentle sisters. But her parents love her just as much as they do their other girls.

Jessica, however, *likes* feeling as though she doesn't fit in. It gives her a reason to rebel, to spend time with her friends instead of her family. Jessica doesn't want to face the hard work it would take to make getting along with her family easier and more enjoyable. So she lies to herself. She exaggerates her misery by closing her eyes to her parents' and sisters' good qualities and emphasizing only the ways in which the family makes her feel different. Soon they're just a problem to her, not real people. Before her senior year, Jessica has already run away from home twice.

What's the payoff of self-deception? It creates a different version of the world, one in which we don't have to work hard on relationships, don't have to take responsibility, and don't have to face challenges.

Of course, self-deception has a major downside. In that world, how you *feel* is more important than any relationship you're in or any commitment you've made. Pretty soon, you find you have a relentless boss (your feelings) running your life—something you'd never put up with from another person! This becomes incredibly stressful. You may feel the wear-and-tear in three areas:

- your relationships—People can't trust you because you live in your own dishonest world.
- your conscience—Eventually, you feel a voice inside calling you back to the world of reality.
- your walk with God—You can't be close to the one you need; you can't sense him, because he doesn't disclose himself to those who walk away from his commands (John 14:21). Lying cuts you off from the strength you need, because it cuts you off from the strength-giver.

How close to the truth are you? I'll guarantee you, the more honest you are, the lower your stress will be. The results of lying (including white lies), shaming, excuse-making, rationalizing, stretching the truth, self-deceit, and misrepresenting reality all create the stress that comes with living in the real world and your own world at the same time. It's like trying to be a citizen of two countries with totally different laws, customs, and languages at the same time. It can't be done, and you'll be stressed out if you try.

Want to lessen your stress and avoid stress in the future? Get real with yourself about your life—and make it a habit. You'll never regret it.

And that's the truth.

FIVE

Knowing Yourself

Angela started attending South Central High three months ago. She's pretty, smart, and already a starter on the girls' basketball team. Angela shouldn't have any trouble fitting in. Still, she's doing everything she can to make sure things go her way.

Since Angela moved to town, two guys, Rob and Mark, have been paying special attention to her. Rob is sweet, considerate, funny, and the kind of guy you can depend on. Mark is a little bit mean-spirited, but he's very popular—rich and good-looking. Angela actually likes Rob better (he's such a good guy, who wouldn't?). But Mark can do more for her. With his influence, he can get her into the best parties and help her hook up with the "in" crowd.

Angela blows off Rob, hurting him badly, and starts dating Mark instead. Within two months, Angela and Mark are fighting, and it's just a matter of time before they break up. But Angela doesn't care. Mark has already given her social life a big boost, and she's sure she can still get Rob to take her out— at least until someone "better" comes along.

What is Angela's problem? Is she just a selfish, mean person? Maybe. But there's another very real possibility. Sometimes people who seem unkind actually *want* to treat others well, but they're afraid they'll be left in the dust if they do. Such people don't realize how much they have going for them just as they are. They believe they have to manipulate or control others to make it in this world. They don't know who they are or why people might like them—and there are few things in this world that cause more stress than that.

Angela doesn't believe she's worth much. Because she thinks no one else will take care of her, she is convinced that she must assert herself as the center of the universe. You probably know "me first" people like this. They are the ones who do everything they can to get their own way. People who act this way are so preoccupied with themselves, they barely recognize the needs of others, if at all. People are important to them only to the degree that they provide what these people want or need.

It's easy to come down hard on Angela for acting this way. But the reality is, we have a tendency to do the same thing. It's the way we were born—part of our old, fallen, sinful nature. If nothing happens to change us, we all will turn out like Angela. But when we come into a relationship with Christ, he changes us. The old self cares only about what we want; the new self cares about what God wants—for us, and for others.

The Bible describes it this way: "For the flesh [the old self] sets its desire against the Spirit, and the Spirit against the flesh; for these are in opposition to one another" (Galatians 5:17, NASB).

The old self's survival methods create a lot of stress. That self will lie, cheat, steal, manipulate, and use people to get ahead. You and I need to figure out how to keep the old self in check, because it's never going to lead us to the good things—the healthy life—God has in store.

How do we do that? By putting up a fight against the selfish desires of our old nature. Think of it this way: To live as a Christian is to do battle. The new self can't be made stronger without a purposeful, daily battle against the old self. One teacher offered this explanation:

> The Christian is a new creature, although the eggshells of the old nature still cling to him. He walks by the Spirit and not in the flesh, even if again and again he is in conflict with the flesh and that means with self-will and a false independence—and must renew the struggle again and again. For participation in the victory of Christ is not merely "believing in it" but standing and living in it—even if as such it is at the same time a resistance-to-evil, a fight.[1]

We are called to fight a good fight. Think *Gladiator*. Think *Braveheart*. Think about any battle you know of in which good ultimately wins over evil. That's the kind of fight you're engaged in every day.

None of us can win this challenge in our own strength. Instead, we must look up to God who directs the battle *by telling us who we are*. When we listen attentively to God, we find four major ways in which he helps us do this: through belonging, giftedness, vision, and passion.

Finding a Sense of Belonging

Angela's problem began because she was so desperate to fit in. She didn't think there was any place where she belonged. In her mind, it was "every man for himself!" No wonder she was stressed out!

Reactions like Angela's are not uncommon. The old self doesn't think about its place in a bigger community. It only thinks about what it wants for itself.

Cameron became a Christian just last year. No one else in his family has ever been to church, so the truth Cameron is learning is new to him. He is learning for the first time how much God loves him, how valuable he is, and how much he has to contribute to the church, his family, and the world. Because of this, Cameron finds himself living a more loving, thoughtful life, as he tries to extend to others the same love God has for him.

Cameron's little brother, Evan, isn't a Christian. That doesn't make Evan any less valuable to God. However, Evan has no idea how important he really is. As a result, he is always trying to *prove* his worth in ineffective ways: by fighting in school, by taking drugs to be popular, by cheating in class in order to get better grades, by bragging. Cameron feels bad for Evan. But he knows his little brother just doesn't get it yet.

Like Evan, the old self tries to look like it's going somewhere by promoting its own self-importance. The old self has no true home.

The new self, on the other hand, has a wonderful place to belong. That place is God's family. The Bible says: "He [God] predestined us to adoption as sons [and daughters] through Jesus Christ to Himself, according to the kind intention of His will" (Ephesians 1:5, NASB). Scripture also tells us: "You are a chosen race, a royal priesthood, a holy nation, a people for God's own possession, that you may proclaim the excellencies of Him who has called you out of darkness into His marvelous light; for you once were not a people, but now you are the people of God" (1 Peter 2:9-10, NASB).

Do you go to church? Some teenagers think of church as being stuffy and boring. But it's actually a great place to connect with God *and* with others. (Besides, church is only as boring as the people who go there, so you have a lot of power to affect this if you go!) There, you'll find teenagers (and adults that care about teens) who are concerned about the things that really matter in life. You'll find people who are committed to loving you and helping you to become the person God created you to be.

In church you'll sense that big things are going on. Lives are being turned around. Prayers are being offered for hurting, persecuted people in lands you may never have heard of before. Parents are called not to provoke their children to anger, but to break through walls of hurt and unforgiveness to love their kids. Children are called to honor their parents. People reach out to the poor and those in prison. The old self is gently but firmly shoved out of the center.

When you have a place to belong, you can be free from the chains of the old self-serving life. In fact, learning to become free is a big part of what the Christian life is about. If you're a Christian, you're already a part of God's family. You just need to start living that way (if you're not already). If you're not a Christian yet, it's as simple as asking Jesus into your heart. He—and the entire family of Christian believers—are waiting to welcome you. Just like that old poster of Uncle Sam says, "We want you!" Really. And God wants you most of all.

STRESSBUSTER:
When was the last time you got out there and worked your body? I'm talking about real exercise. Learning to make physical activity a part of your everyday life is one of the best things you can do to de-stress. When you train your body to deal with physical stress (exercise), you help it learn how to better deal with other kinds of stress. Not only that, exercise helps you stay in shape, which is just good for your body all around and helps you avoid those same diseases we've been talking about: heart disease, high blood pressure, etc.

What's your exercise of choice? Do you like to run? Walk your dog? Play laser tag with your friends? Rollerblade? Ride your bike? Experts recommend thirty minutes of physical activity per day, alternating with more vigorous activity at least three times a week. Don't let your busy schedule crowd out physical exercise, and you'll notice a result both in your stress level and in the way your mind and body feel.

Embracing Your Giftedness

One of the more stunning verses in the New Testament tells us that when Jesus ascended into heaven, he "gave gifts to men" (Ephesians 4:8, NASB). Not only do we have our freedom in Christ, Jesus has given gifts to each of us. That includes *you!* You may not know what your gifts are yet, but I guarantee that you have them. Finding them, and learning to use them, will help you make a difference in the world, and in the body of Christ.

God's main gift to us is the Holy Spirit, who helps us learn how to use the other gifts God has given us. When Jesus left earth and went back to heaven, he knew we'd need someone to help us down here. So he sent us the Holy Spirit, whom he describes by saying, "I will pray to the Father, and He will give you another Helper, that He may abide with you forever, even the Spirit of truth, whom the world cannot receive, because it neither sees Him nor knows Him; but you know Him, for He dwells with you and will be in you" (John 14:16-17, NKJV).

Besides the Holy Spirit, God has also given us individual talents and gifts. Some of those gifts are named in Scripture; some are not. In 1 Corinthians 12:1 (NASB), the apostle Paul says: "Now concerning spiritual gifts, brethren, I do not want you to be unaware." A few verses later, he goes on to list some of those gifts he wants us to know about.

Now there are varieties of gifts, but the same Spirit. And there are varieties of ministries, and the same Lord. And there are varieties of effects, but the same God who works all things in all persons. But to each one is given the manifestation of the Spirit for the common good. For to one is given the word of wisdom through the Spirit, and to another the word of knowledge according to the same Spirit; to another faith by the same Spirit, and to another gifts of healing by the one Spirit, and to another the effecting of miracles, and to another prophecy, and to another the distinguishing of spirits, to another various kinds of tongues, and to another the interpretation of tongues. But one and the same Spirit works all these things, distributing to each one individually just as He wills.

1 CORINTHIANS 12:4-11, NASB

Some gifts are supernatural abilities that bring about incredible spiritual results. Other gifts are natural, inborn talents God stirred into you in your mother's womb. The list of gifts in 1 Corinthians 12, given above, is probably suggestive, rather than exhaustive. For example, this list doesn't include strong math skills, the ability to throw a football, or having an ear for singing harmony, but those are all God-given gifts, too. No matter what your gifts, God will give you a place to use them. Whether the gifts we receive are supernatural abilities or natural talents, it is God's desire that we use them to serve his kingdom.

Ever since she was in seventh grade, Renee had had a hard time in school. One of her legs was shorter than the other, so she walked a little funny. It didn't matter to the other kids that she was good-looking, had a great sense of humor, and was good at writing. They only saw that she was different, and they teased her mercilessly for it.

During this time, Renee's "old self" took over. Trying to survive in her own strength, she felt justified in arguing, picking on those who were weaker than she was, and being lazy at home. At times, her behavior was as ugly as the treatment she received at school.

In high school, things got better. After Renee started attending a local church, the youth pastor and his wife took her under their wing. Before long, Renee began to discover her gifts of mercy and her love of the written word. As these and other gifts blossomed, she started to see that she was much more than what she had believed herself to be. She was set free by her thankfulness for God's gifts and decided that if God had given them to her, he would find a place where she could use them. Rather than being stressed out, she could trust in God's purposes, relax, and enjoy finding out what he had planned for her.

Like Renee, you have incredible gifts. They may not feel like much yet, but they are an important part of who you are, and in time—especially as you seek to live out and share those gifts—you too will begin to see what an extraordinary person God has created you to be!

STRESSBUSTER:
What do you like to do when you have time to yourself? Make a list of five things. Now, when was the last time you did each one? If you don't know, or if remembering how long it's been makes you depressed, it's time to get more fun back into your life! Consider whether your course

load is too much right now. If your classes are too hard or too advanced, talk to a parent or counselor about it. Maybe you need to drop that part-time job so you can focus on your schoolwork and *still* have time for yourself.

Whether you enjoy playing tennis or singing in the school musical, writing poetry or riding dirt bikes, make sure you have time to blow off some steam and stress by doing the things you love!

Catching a New Vision

As we discover our gifts, a vision begins to grow inside us. One young person who had a vision for her God-given gifts was Rachel Scott. Rachel was killed when two students entered Colorado's Columbine High School in 1999 and killed thirteen of their classmates.

Before her death, Rachel wrote in an essay: "I have this theory that if one person can go out of their way to show compassion, then it will start a chain reaction of the same."[2] Friends and family remember Rachel as being one of the most compassionate people they'd ever known, and today they continue to try to follow her example.

Rachel saw that, through her gift of compassion, she could start a chain reaction of God-centered compassion in those around her. That gift gave her a vision, helping her to see possibilities, potential, and opportunities where she'd seen nothing before.

In Ephesians 4:22-24 (NASB), the Bible calls us to "lay aside the old self, which is being corrupted in accordance with the lusts of deceit, and that you be renewed in the spirit of your mind, and put on the new self, which in the likeness of God has been created in righteousness and holiness of the truth." God is talking about a process by which we watch for old-self strategies and cut them off whenever they show up.

Lying to others to get what we want? Not an option. Gossiping about friends, so that we look better in comparison? No way. We don't need to act this way anymore. We can take God up on his offer of a whole new way of thinking and feeling. But to strengthen the new, we have to say "No" to the old.

Don't think you can do it on your own? Don't worry. As you turn to God, he will equip you to discover and use your gifts as you live out a life that's marked by love for God and lived out with incredible passion.

Living With Passion

Passion? Aren't teenagers supposed to be on guard against passion? Yes and no. Sexual passion, while very normal, can also be very dangerous for teenagers. But that's not the kind of passion I'm talking about. I'm referring to the kind of passion that makes you excited about the future—the kind of passion that makes you grab onto life with both hands and live for all you're worth.

Some people believe that the Christian life is supposed to be dull, boring, and predictable. Nothing could be further from the truth! Passion means that every day, the Christian life is more and more of a holy thrill.

Author John Eldredge says, "The gospel will either take your breath away, or something else will."[3] He's right. We all are created to live passionate lives. If our God and the Christian life don't inspire passion and excitement in us, we're going to go find other things—unhealthy things like drugs, sex, and crime—that will (only temporarily).

No matter what you think you want, God will send you what you need the most. Whatever good comes to you comes from him. No matter how things look at the time, God always wants the best for you—and he's the only one around who can provide it.

Here's the good news: Either God is going to give you exactly what you want, or he's going to give you something much better. What does that mean to your life today? It means that you can go ahead and can live life with excitement and passion, because you can trust what you're going to receive. That doesn't mean hard times won't come. They're a part of life, too. But those hard times will ultimately make you stronger. They will make you a better, more compassionate, more loving person. And hard times won't last forever.

STRESSBUSTER:

Do you have at least one close friend you can talk to? Someone with whom you can share your insecurities, fears, and struggles? Girls often connect with others successfully, but boys can suffer from the misconception that guys are supposed to "have it all together." The truth is, no one is free from struggle, and pretending otherwise only stresses us out.

Don't forget, you need close friends who know what's going on in your life. If you don't have some, make a determined effort to get to know other teens in your school, neighborhood, or church. You need them—and they need you! As you get to know each other better, test the waters by gradually sharing your feelings with one another. If the person is safe, keep sharing. You may end up making one of the best friends of your life!

Putting It All Together

Belonging. Giftedness. Vision. Passion. These are the four pillars of your strong, new self. Through each of these areas, God answers your crucial, heartfelt questions. Whatever you need, whatever your fears, doubts, and longings, God is right next to you, just waiting for you to ask so he can answer you.

Our growth in Christ comes as we go deeper and deeper into our questions. As God helps us answer them, we become anchored to someone and something solid: Hope. We begin to trust his promises more and more as our new self grows and blossoms.

The world is full of stress. But as you come to know yourself as the gifted person God designed you to be, you'll have more resources to draw from in times of stress. You'll see that you *do* have great worth and you *can* make a difference in this world—starting right now, exactly where you are.

How's *that* for lightening your stress load?

SIX

Finding Rest

Josie has never been so exhausted in her life. Between band practice, play practice, homework, and her social life, she's barely getting six hours of sleep a night. The result? She practically sleeps through the first few classes of the day, waking up only in time for lunch. After lunch, the blood travels from Josie's brain to her stomach and she feels more tired than ever. Her teachers are frustrated with her and often complain that she doesn't pay attention in class. But how can she when she's ready to fall asleep at any minute?

Slow Down, You're Moving Too Fast

Author Paul Tournier wrote, "The yield of our life does not depend so much on the number of things that we do, but more on the quality of self-giving that we put into each thing."[1] How well are you taking care of yourself? Don't know? That's no surprise. After all, in this busy world, when have you ever had time to think about it?

The world we live in is like a training compound for the busy, and for busy-wannabes. Our world screams like a red-faced drill instructor, "Go faster! Do more! Think quicker!" Learning to rest is a huge stressbuster, but it's not easy to learn how.

A lot of high school yearbooks include interesting little phrases under people's pictures. Some might say, "Most likely to succeed" or "Most likely to make a million dollars." If you look into it, you'll find that usually the people who *do* the most (engage in the most extracurricular activities) get most of the "attaboys" and "attagirls" under their pictures. But those activities aren't really a very good measuring stick for their strengths—or yours.

When you apply to a college, the admissions officer generally asks you about your grades, your test scores, and your activities. Can you imagine a college application that asked, "How strong are your meditation habits?" or "How much time do you spend in prayer?" Almost nowhere in our society are you encouraged to pull away from activities in order to put your feet up and do some quiet reflecting. And that's a shame. Because doing this will go a long way in helping us grow as people, and in helping us to bust our stress!

Even when we turn to the spiritual side of life, we're faced with the burden of activity. Churches weigh us by the number of meetings we attend, the number of quiet times we have, the number of times we share our faith, the number of Bible studies we go to. It's all: do, do, do. This reminds me of a teenager who grew up in a super-busy family who said, "Sometimes, I feel like a human doing instead of a human being." But how do we go from frantic "doing" to getting the rest we need?

STRESS 101:

In the 1930s, Dr. Hans Selye (whom we talked about briefly in the introduction) "discovered" stress in a very interesting and unique way: by being a klutz.

Dr. Robert Sapolsky relates the story in *Why Zebras Don't Get Ulcers: A Guide to Stress, Stress-Related Diseases, and Coping.* As the story goes, Dr. Selye was studying the effect of a particular extract on laboratory rats. Every day, he would attempt to inject the rats with the extract, but things didn't go smoothly. "Selye would try to inject the rats, miss them, drop them, spend half the morning chasing the rats around the room or vice versa, flailing with a broom to get them out from behind the sink, and so on."* He also had a control group (a group of rats who did not receive the extract, with whom he compared the effects on his test rats) that he also handled, dropped, and chased. Ultimately, *both* sets of rats developed peptic ulcers, enlarged adrenal glands, and atrophied tissues of the immune system. What did Dr. Selye discover? The rats were stressed out over the way he handled them! From this unusual (and rather ridiculous) experience, Dr. Selye developed the theory of the stress syndrome, and he will forever be known as the man who "discovered" stress.

* Robert M. Sapolsky, *Why Zebras Don't Get Ulcers* (New York: W.H. Freeman, 1994 and 1998), 9.

Receiving God's Call to Rest

We don't have to look too far to see what God has to say on the subject. Isaiah 30:15 (NASB) is an unmistakable call to rest: "In repentance and rest you shall be saved, in quietness and trust is your strength."

Why is God concerned that we rest? Because when we rev up and stay hyper—doing everything busily in our own strength—we can't hear him. I'll say it again: only a quiet heart can know God. His concern that we rest is woven throughout Scripture.

Here are three pictures of rest the Bible paints for us.

The Light Yoke

In Matthew 11:28-30 Jesus says, "Come to me, all you who are loaded down with burdens, and I will give you rest. Take my yoke upon you and learn from me, for I am gentle and humble in heart; and you shall find rest for your souls. For my yoke is easy, and my burden is light" (my paraphrase).

At first, it seems strange that Jesus says to take off the yoke of the world, then put on *his* yoke. Who wants a yoke at all? But when Jesus says, "My yoke is easy," he means that his teaching doesn't weigh us down.[2] The teaching of the religious leaders of Jesus' day weighed the people down with a heavy yoke of rules and requirements. The whole system exhausted people; there was no life in it.

Jesus is saying that his teaching will be easy to carry, because as we learn from him, we find intimacy with a gentle and humble Lord and friend rather than a tyrant who buries us under a load of rules. Anxious rule-keeping keeps us separated from God; Jesus' yoke brings us *into* a relationship with God. He brings rest to that deep place inside that has been anxious and angry.

The Kingdom of God

We've already talked in an earlier chapter about the fact that, as a Christian, you belong in God's kingdom. But what does this mean?

One way God describes his kingdom is that it's a place where he laughs at the movers and shakers of this world. Psalm 2:2 (NASB) says, "The kings of the earth take their stand ... against the Lord and against His [Messiah]." Two verses later, we get God's response: "He who sits in the heavens laughs, the Lord scoffs at them." The leader of our kingdom is the Lord who laughs at the so-called powers of those who think they rule on earth. God knows they're pretending. They're propped up by dishonest claims and feelings of self-importance. But God is not a pretender. He's the real King, and we are tucked away, safe and sound, in his domain, never to be in real danger again.

The Sabbath

Forget those old books and movies about Puritans grimly forbidding any fun on the Sabbath (they're not historically accurate, anyway). The Sabbath is more about a particular attitude than observing a particular day of the week (although that part's important, too). The attitude comes from the fact that in Hebrew, "Sabbath" means "stop."

Sabbath is about coming to a halt and not working. It's about trusting that even when we stop working, God doesn't stop taking care of us. It's about trusting that, since God is not limited by time, we can stop stretching our time, trying to make it do more than it's supposed to do. Time is a created thing, just like we are. We torture it beyond its creaturely limits when we try to multiply it, increase it, extend it. We should respect time by stopping for awhile and allowing ourselves to cease to be productive. That's how we remind ourselves that life doesn't depend on increased activity, but rather on increased intimacy with God.

The light yoke. The kingdom of God. The Sabbath. In all these God beckons. "Follow me," he says, "and I'll take you to a resting place." There, he speaks to our souls and listens to the noise in our hearts.

Decoding the Heart-Noise

Do you have heart-noise? Most of us do. This is the clamor of concerns, questions, and problems that simmer beneath the surfaces of our lives, constantly nagging us, and constantly being ignored. The important thing is not to shove those noises way down out of your awareness.

Last year, Laura took a road trip with her older sister across the state. After they had gone more than halfway, a terrible noise started coming from Laura's engine. The girls had almost no money, so they dealt with the problem the only way they knew how: they turned up the radio and kept driving! Unfortunately for them, the problem could not be ignored, and pretty soon they were on the side of the road, calling home on their cell phone, asking for the number of their dad's AAA card.

Just like car engines, our hearts make "noises" to tell us

when something is wrong. Like Laura, we may be tempted to try to drown them out, especially if we don't feel prepared to do anything about the problem. We may turn up the TV, computer game, or other gadget. But this won't work for long, and the noise will only come back louder. There is one place to go with heart-noise and that is the silence that belongs to God.

This idea comes from the following verse: "Be still, and know that I am God" (Psalm 46:10, NIV). To put it bluntly, God is inviting us—gently, lovingly, but firmly—to pipe down for awhile.

He knows that we distract ourselves and others with our words, worry, and complaints. Talking makes us feel powerful. Author Richard Foster said, "One reason we can hardly bear to remain silent is that it makes us feel so helpless."[3] But we need the helplessness of being quiet. That's the only way we find the help that comes from listening to God. Rather than shoving our heart-noise downward or trying to drown it out with world-noise, we need to take time for quiet. When we do, we let the heart-noise rise to the surface where we learn what it has to tell us and offer to God what we discovered in it.

STRESSBUSTER:
Every person who feels stress (remember, that's *all* of us) needs time to rest. Unfortunately, teens are famous for not getting enough sleep. Teens often stay up late, studying, talking with friends, watching TV, working, or even worrying.

If you don't get enough sleep, however, you're going to be stressed. That lack of sleep will also negatively impact your performance in school and your ability to relate to others. Here are a few strategies to help you catch up on your zzzzz's:

1. *Cut the caffeine.* Soft drinks and coffee are loaded with caffeine, as is chocolate. If you're buzzed on caffeine at night, you'll have a harder time getting to sleep.

2. *Catch a catnap.* A quick nap in the afternoon can help you recharge in time for an evening of studying, working, or playing.

3. *Get to bed earlier.* Can't miss that favorite TV show? That's what VCRs are for! Tape it and watch it later if you still really want to.

Fighting the Activity Culture

Remember Josie, at the beginning of this chapter? You've probably felt like her at times: harried, exhausted, frantic, and so worn out you're unable to think.

The modern world is like a reform school for turning happy tortoises into frantic hares. It teaches us "that the most important thing in this world is to be strong."[4] Busy-ness and strength are the keys to success, according to the world.

But what does the Bible say? "When I am weak, then I am strong" (2 Corinthians 12:10, NASB). By "weak," Scripture doesn't mean wimpy; it means a willingness to admit our need for God. How can we fight this hyper-drive activity culture of ours? Two ways.

First, as often as you can, get away from your computer and TV. Why? Because they usually bring you messages that tell you to speed up. They speed you up by making you less content with yourself, your parents, your life, your home, your possessions, your siblings, your school, your decisions, and more. A technologically advanced life isn't usually a very restful life, and eventually this will take its toll on you in stress.

Second, take a serious look at your friends. We experience great stress when we link our identity primarily to our friends' opinions of us.

When my friends act as my mirror, I've just given up enormous power. I've made myself more dependent on people than on God.

Instead of making our friends into emotional supply hoses, God wants us talking to *him* inside our hearts all day long (1 Thessalonians 5:17 (NASB) says, "Pray without ceasing"). When we do this, we can *give* to our friends rather than anxiously snatching at the crumbs they might throw our way.

God says he will "never leave you or forsake you." He is the friend that "loves at all times." He calls us to tank up on his love. Learning to be quiet and tank up on God's love—that's true rest.

SEVEN

Dealing With Confusing Adults

I'm heading over to Charlie's house!" John yells over his shoulder as he heads out the door. "Can I stay for dinner?"

John's mother calls to him from the kitchen. "If his mother says it's okay." But she and John both know it will be fine. Charlie's mom is always thrilled to have John stay and eat with her boys. "Just be back by eight."

John couldn't be happier. It's barely three-thirty. That gives him four and a half hours to hang out with his best friend. When he gets to Charlie's house, however, Charlie's little sister meets him at the door.

"Mom and Charlie are at his soccer game," she informs John.

"But I was supposed to come over." John can't help glaring at her a little bit.

Angie shrugs. "What can I say? He had a make-up game. Guess he should have called you."

John grumbles to himself. Charlie *should* have called him. But he's not really mad. Just disappointed.

He hops back onto his bike and pedals furiously home. As he enters the back door, he lets the screen slam shut behind him.

"John? Is that you?" His mom comes out of the kitchen. Her eyes are glassy, and she looks angry. "What are you doing here?"

John stares at her in surprise. "Charlie wasn't home after all."

"Well, you two had better get your stories straight!" She's practically screeching at him now. "And what are you doing, slamming the screen like that? How many times do I have to tell you not to do that? Go to your room. I just can't handle you right now!"

"But, Mom ..."

"Now!"

John goes. But he's confused. His mom gets like this sometimes. One minute she'll be fine, the next she goes berserk.

John knows that his mom has unpredictable moods. What he doesn't know is that she has a drinking problem. In fact, she started drinking the minute he walked out the door, thinking she'd have plenty of time to sober up before he got home. Now, she's been caught. She's embarrassed, angry—and taking it out on John.

STRESSBUSTER:

There is absolutely nothing more stressful than being the victim of abuse. If you are being abused sexually, physically, or emotionally, tell someone immediately. Talk with a parent, a friend's parent, a teacher, a counselor, a pastor, or some other adult you trust. Know that by law they *have* to report certain kinds of abuse, but that there are adults out there who can protect you. Ask God to lead you to the adults who can help. If for any reason you don't get results, don't give up! Go to another adult for help. If you know a friend is being abused, seek help for him or her as well. They need your friendship now more than ever.

Who Are You, and What Have You Done With the Person I Love?

We know that teenagers experience stress. But adults also have stress and problems of their own. Sometimes they're exhausted and entangled in troubles. Unless they work hard to solve their problems constructively, their behavior can be hard to handle.

Confusing behavior by adults can be caused by any number of different problems. One is embarrassment. Sometimes, there are subjects about which adults feel ashamed (for example, drinking, going bald, gaining weight, how much money they make, their religious beliefs, why Aunt Becky is always sick, why Uncle George is no longer part of the family, etc.). The problem is, it's hard to know exactly what the embarrassing subjects are. Being in the dark like this can give you the feeling that you're walking around in a minefield. John, for example, was clueless about his mother's drinking problem. Even when he did see the signs, he worked hard to deny that whiff of alcohol he smelled on her breath.

Families can also keep secrets that don't surface for generations. For example, my great-grandfather left my great-grandmother around 1920, a time when divorce was almost unheard of. One of his two daughters, my grandmother, was so angry and ashamed of what he'd done, she considered him dead. By her own choice, she never saw him again.

Later, when she had two kids of her own, one of whom became my father, she told them their grandfather was dead. My father was twenty-two when he discovered that his grand-father had been alive until my dad was sixteen. He was furious with his mother over her choice to hide the truth from him. Their relationship never healed, and the anger he felt toward her permanently damaged his view of women. To him, they were controlling and devious. His mistrust of women played a significant part in my parents' divorcing when I was nineteen.

Embarrassment and secrets are just two of many reasons adults act in confusing ways. When their behavior confuses you, you can use the following tactics to help you cope with your stress.

GOD ON STRESS:
"The Lord is good, a refuge in times of trouble. He cares for those who trust in him" (Nahum 1:7, NIV).

Bring God Into It

No matter how much they love you and want the best for you, adults don't always behave in ways that make you feel loved. When this happens, it's easy to think, "There must be something wrong with me, or she wouldn't be acting this way." But that isn't the truth. Adults—whether they're your parents, teachers, coaches, youth group leaders, aunts or uncles, or other grown-ups in your life—can be grumpy, crabby, and just plain selfish, just like you and I can. Sometimes there's a clear reason for their behavior, and sometimes there isn't. Either way, it isn't your fault.

Remember, although grown-ups do make mistakes, there's someone you can turn to who is always trustworthy. That's God. God won't ever mistreat you—accidentally *or* on purpose. He's completely reliable. When you feel like your world is spinning out of control, turn to the one who is truly in control. Tell him how you feel. Picture him wrapping his arms around you, because that's exactly what he's doing. You can always trust in him, no matter what the behavior of the grown-ups around you.

STRESSBUSTER:
Take out a blank sheet of paper, and at the top write: "Things that aren't confusing about God." For example, you could write: "God loves me," "He keeps his promises," "He wants my good," and so on. What you're trying to do is increase your sense of living in God's embrace at all times. Even though the adults in your world may become confusing, God is still the one who says, "Come unto me all you who are weary and loaded down, and I will give you rest" (Matthew 11:28, my paraphrase).

Admit You're Confused
When things don't make sense we often try to make sense of them by placing the blame the one place we feel we can: on ourselves. Don't try to let anyone off the hook that easily.

For example, John could have reflected, "Well, I guess I

should have called Charlie to make sure he was home." This is not a good direction for John to take, because it moves the issue away from what's true ("I'm confused; I don't understand Mom") to what's untrue ("Mom's behavior must be my fault"). In the long run, it's always less stressful to deal with the truth, even when the truth is painful.

State the Facts

If it feels safe to do so, make a matter-of-fact, non-smart-alecky statement like, "Mom, you're really confusing me right now" or "I really feel bad about what you said when I came in the door." This lets the adults in your world know that their behavior makes an impact on you. Over a period of time, they may be influenced to take more responsibility for their behavior. Then again, they may not. But it's important—without forming harsh accusations—to make your feelings gently, but firmly, known.

Fight Fair

Just as you should not attack yourself ("this *must* be my fault"), it's important that you don't attack the adult in your life. If John yells at his mother, "I can't *believe* you think it's okay to abuse your kids," you can be sure that she will respond with further harshness. Then the two of them will be in a struggle where there has to be a winner and a loser. Win/lose battles are very stressful because love can't really be a part of them. If you're trying to win or trying hard not to lose, you can't convey love to the other person.

You may not feel a lot of love at the time, but Jesus calls us to love everyone, including our enemies, and love is the only thing that can bring peace, reconciliation, and real hope into our lives. Luckily, love isn't just a feeling. It's a choice. You can choose to act in a loving way. Often, the feelings follow afterward.

Stand Up for Yourself

At times, you may find that you need to assert, or defend, yourself, though you must do so while treating the other person with the utmost respect. Earl Hipp, a writer on teen stress, says that, "assertiveness is a skill."[1] Hipp's approach to assertiveness is explained as a six-step process represented by the acronym A.S.S.E.R.T.:

- The **"A"** stands for "Attention." Before you can work on a problem you're having with another person, you first have to get the person to agree to listen to you.
- The **"S"** stands for "Soon, Simple, Short." Unless you're too upset to be clear about your feelings, try to respond as soon as you realize that your rights have been violated. That way, the circumstances will still be fresh for everyone. State the problem simply and briefly.
- The second **"S"** stands for "Specific Behavior." Focus on the behavior of the person you're having trouble with. Don't focus on how you feel about the person.
- The **"E"** stands for "Effect on Me." Help the person to understand the feelings and problems you are experiencing as a result of his or her behavior.
- The **"R"** stands for "Response." Describe what you need for the relationship to work—the changed behavior

that would help you to get along better. Then ask the other person for feedback on your request.

- The **"T"** stands for "Terms." If all goes well, you should be able to work out an agreement about how to handle similar situations in the future.[2]

Forgive the Confusing Person

One of the all-time best things about Jesus is that he forgave you and me the very worst things we've done. It's tempting to want to forgive people only when they're *really* sorry, but that's not how it works. The more we hold a grudge and the longer we refuse to forgive others, the easier it is to become bitter. That only hurts us—not the confusing adult who caused the problem in the first place.

Often, it's scary to be confused, so we turn that confusion into anger in an attempt to feel more powerful. This, too, will only hurt you.

Don't gossip with your friends about the person. This is a natural temptation, especially when you've allowed yourself to stay angry and not forgive. Your friends may unknowingly feed your bitterness by saying things like, "Yeah, my mom's a jerk, too." This just makes things worse.

Everyone has good qualities and bad qualities. The more you can focus on the good qualities of the person you need to forgive, and the more you can believe that painful situations in their own life have influenced them to act the way they do, the closer you will come to a solution to your situation.

Seek Help

If you think the confusing person in your life is dangerous, talk to an adult you can trust. Get help. Uneasiness about an adult should not be ignored. If someone is making you feel creepy, uncomfortable, or threatened, don't keep it to yourself.

Whom can you trust? Admittedly, trustworthy people can be hard to find. But there *are* many caring people out there who will want to help you. Here are some ideas: (a) Your parents. Unless one or both of your parents are making you feel uncomfortable, tell them about the adult who makes you uneasy. (b) An aunt, uncle, or older brother or sister, whom you really trust. (c) Your pastor or youth pastor. (d) The director of your local Christian-run Crisis Pregnancy Center. (e) If you are being physically or sexually abused, call your local police station. Ask for Victims Services: this is a branch of law enforcement aimed at protecting those who are being abused by someone more powerful than they.

Hope Is Ahead

At the beginning of this chapter, John had been banished to his room for almost catching his mom drinking. After praying about it, he decides to call his pastor.

After a day of phone tag, he gets in touch with his pastor and describes the situation. They discuss it awhile and decide that the pastor will visit John's mom as part of an effort the church has been making to stay in better contact with those who visit the church only occasionally.

The pastor doesn't want to put John in the uncomfortable

position of being in the middle, so he says he'll bring a brochure the church provides, to use as a conversation starter. John's mom will be given a printed checklist of needs and asked to pick her top five. The pastor is hoping she'll check the one that says, "I need to know more about breaking destructive habits." If she does, he can start working with her on her drinking right away. If she doesn't, he'll still have five areas in which he and the church can start ministering to her. In time, once she feels safe with the pastor and the church, she may admit to someone that she has a problem with alcohol.

Meanwhile, the pastor makes sure John gets in touch with a member of his youth staff who will meet regularly with John and keep their discussions confidential. Eventually, the pastor helps John get involved with a support group for children of alcoholics.

John's problem doesn't go away immediately. It is unlikely that his mom will instantly get better. But there are things he can do to relieve some of the stress caused by her behavior.

The same thing is true for you. No matter what mixed messages you get from the adults in your life—no matter who they are—you are worthwhile, you do have hope, and God will bring you help to get you through the hardest times.

That's one thing you don't have to be confused about.

EIGHT

Beating School Stress

Fifteen-year-old Jody wakes up to the buzz of her alarm clock and smashes the "snooze" button. She settles back against her pillow. *Ugh.* She barely slept at all. She has three tests today, and she hasn't had time enough to study adequately for any of them. Not to mention the fact that her best friend, Rachel, has been giving her a hard time because she doesn't think Jody has been spending enough time with her. But how can she? Between schoolwork and Jody's job at the local taco joint, she barely has a social life at all. Now, on top of everything else, the school has been warning the kids that a new metal detector is going to be installed, because several kids have been caught with knives—usually on the street where Jody parks her car. She's worried about flunking her tests, losing her friend, and getting knifed.

When Jody goes down to breakfast, her dad looks at her ruefully over the paper. "What's with the glum face?" he asks. "You think *your* life is hard? I wish I was a teenager again. I wish my life was that easy."

Jody stares at him, hardly believing what she's hearing. *Is he kidding?*

Every teenager knows that school is a major source of stress. Giving eight hours a day to an educational institution is definitely a drain on your time, but it's also a drain on your heart. Even the best school situation puts a strain on the mind and emotions. In this chapter, we'll look at three common sources of school stress: academic pressure, peer hassles, and worries about violence. All three can affect your life negatively, but by doing some stressbusting, you can bring your stress back down to a manageable level, where it belongs.

The Squeeze of Academics

Academic pressure often comes from three sources: (1) the schools themselves, as they seek to raise end-of-grade test scores (and thus maintain their academic reputation); (2) colleges and universities as they offer dire warnings about the difficulty of qualifying for admission; (3) parents who are anxious because of the above two reasons, and/or because they measure their own success as parents by the grades their teens make.

Let's look at these problems one by one. First, the school. You know this already, but let me take this opportunity to remind you of an important truth: your school's reputation isn't your responsibility or problem. The best reason to go to school is to learn. Period. Every bit of information you gain goes into your mind and helps you become the person God intends you to be.

Other people may be stressed out for their own reasons, but you don't have to let them pass that stress on to you. It doesn't matter if your school is the best one in the district. What matters is that you are getting something good and solid out of your education. That doesn't always show up on test scores, but it will show up in your life.

Then there is the pressure that comes from colleges and universities. Keep in mind, they want you to come to their school, because students are what keep their school going. They're going to do what they can to help you. Yes, you need to fill out your applications, take your SATs, and fulfill other requirements. But there's no need to have a meltdown. Do your best. Pray about the results. Then trust God with the outcome. You don't have to stress out when he's on your side.

The third problem is the issue of parental stress. One high school freshman lamented, "My dad says if I'm going to get into med school, I need to be making straight A's *now*. That means I have to study all the time. I have no life!"

As I write, I have two daughters in high school and a daughter in college. The two high schoolers feel far greater pressure than my collegian. They say that their school is full of pressure and anxiety. Teachers don't feel they can take the time to stop and answer random student questions, because they have to focus solely on material covered in end-of-the-year tests. Since everyone moves along at a breakneck speed, many students end up with a poor grasp of a wide scope of material instead of a firm grasp of a narrower, but still respectable slice of the subject.

Often, neither teachers nor administrators can answer the question, "Why should I kill myself to make the grade?" The answers that come usually just put off the "Why?" question a bit longer. Here's an example:

"You should make good grades so you can get into a good university."
"Why?"

"So you can get into med school or law school or vet school or business school."

"Why?"

"So you could earn a good living and provide for your family."

"But then won't I be in the same situation I'm in now? Only then, my kids will be the ones asking *me* 'Why?' What will I tell them?"

"Um ... next question."

Unless there is a real reason for getting an education (and in the above chain of reasons, no life-sustaining reason is given), the stress of education will seem like a tiresome climb up a staircase that leads nowhere.

The only way out of this impasse is to explore the importance of belonging, giftedness, vision, and passion—concepts we covered in chapter five. Education that's not set in a context of greater meaning (such as service to God's kingdom) will not only be stressful but will promote cynicism. But when you see your education as something that can help you achieve great things and become the unique person only you can be, you'll have solid, low-stress motivation to learn, and to use what you learn to make a difference in the world.

Peer Hassles: Establishing Boundaries

I debated about whether to call this section "Peer Pressure" or not, and I decided against it. Peer pressure is such an overused term, people don't even hear it anymore ("Oh yeah, peer pressure. That's when parents say, 'If everybody jumped off a bridge, would you do it, too?'"). I chose the phrase "Peer Hassles," because when I talk to teens about their peers, I hear them talking about something bigger than peer pressure. I hear them talking about their friends wanting more from them than they can reasonably provide. Here are some things teens often want from each other:

- total affirmation: "Tell me I'm good and never stop telling me."
- total acceptance: "No matter what I do—cheat off your paper, steal from you, lie to you, get you in trouble through my addictive behavior—I want you to always give me approval."
- total availability: "I don't want you to have any other friends besides me. Or, if you do have other friends (which I won't like), you must call me your best friend and let everyone know that's what I am."

There's nothing wrong with wanting affirmation, acceptance, and availability. But none of us is able to provide all the affirmation, acceptance, and availability our friends need. When our friends start asking for more than we can give, we experience a *lot* of stress. Why? Because in a sense, what they are doing is asking us to be God for them—and that's a job we just can't do.

Don't get me wrong. We are, in a sense, God's hands and feet on this earth. We are supposed to demonstrate his love to others. But ultimately, they must find their hope, comfort, safety, and strength in him, not in us. When our friends pressure us to fill God's place in their lives, we feel smothered. We may wind up hating ourselves for not being enough, or hating them for asking too much.

Bottom line: Teens need to have boundaries with each other. Boundaries are major stressbusters. What are boundaries? Limits. When you set limits, life is less stressful.

Picture your life as a room with a door, through which people can come in and out.[1] When you respect yourself, the doorknob is on the *inside* of the room. When you lack self-respect, the doorknob is on the *outside*. Others can yank the door open and come in and out as they please. You need to make sure you keep the doorknob on the inside.

What does this look like in real life? When you establish boundaries, you make sure other people can't tell you how to think, feel, or act. You can care about other people's feelings and wants, and you *should*. But ultimately, how you live your life and what you choose to do are up to you.

You create boundaries in three areas: physical, intellectual, and emotional.[2] When you have healthy *physical boundaries*, you have a feeling for the difference between unhealthy and healthy touch. You can move away from people who stand too close or crowd you as they're talking.

When you have healthy *intellectual boundaries*, you can claim your opinions and ideas as your own, even when others don't like them. You can (and should) be respectful of what they think and feel, but you don't have to give up what you think and feel just because they want you to. Others should assume that the only expert on what you think is you.

When you have healthy *emotional boundaries*, you don't apologize for your feelings just because someone else finds them inconvenient. You don't let your emotions run your life, but you do listen to your feelings and try to understand what they're telling you. You don't let others overload you with their feelings, although you care about their happiness or distress. You are compassionate toward them, but you realize that, in the end, they're responsible for their feelings just as you are for yours.

Boundaries are about choosing what you'll tolerate and what you won't, which means *not* being passive. (Instead of saying "I know it was wrong, but she was so lonely and persuasive," you say "I allowed her loneliness to influence me, and I shouldn't have. I let her choose for me.")

GOD ON STRESS:

"Therefore I [Jesus] tell you, do not worry about your life, what you will eat or drink; or about your body, what you will wear. Is not life more important than food, and the body more important than clothes? Look at the birds of the air; they do not sow or reap or store away in barns, and yet your heavenly Father feeds them. Are you not much more valuable than they? Who of you by worrying can add a single hour to his life? And why do you worry about clothes? See how the lilies of the field grow. They do not labor or spin. Yet I tell you that not even Solomon in all his splendor was dressed like one of these. If that is how God clothes the grass of the field, which is here today and tomorrow is thrown into the fire, will he not much more clothe you, O you of little faith? So do not worry, saying, 'What shall we eat?' or 'What shall we drink?' or 'What shall we wear?' For the pagans run after all these things, and your heavenly Father knows that you need them. But seek first his kingdom and his righteousness, and all these things will be given to you as well. Therefore do not worry about tomorrow, for tomorrow will worry about itself. Each day has enough trouble of its own" (Matthew 6:25-34, NIV).

Dreading School Violence

A teenager told me recently, "They just took down the fence around my high school. Now we have no security, and I worry about just anybody getting on campus and about getting hurt."

Violence on school campuses has never been a bigger issue than it is today. Some of the security measures used in schools actually make students feel unsafe, because they remind them of potential danger. Other students feel frightened because they don't think there is *enough* security at their schools.

Unfortunately, school violence is an issue that doesn't seem to be going away. In light of that, what can you do to lower your stress? Here are a few ideas.

Choose Safe Friends

Did you know that hanging out with high-risk kids increases your chances of experiencing violence? Kids who drink and do drugs are usually kids who don't cope well with their own anger. Never having learned how to handle anger, they're more likely to let it out in harmful ways. Do you want to be around for that? This goes back to what we talked about earlier: the importance of choosing safe people in your life.

Where can you turn to find more safe people to hang out with? Many schools have Christian programs like Young Life where kids can find a place to belong without having to accept destructive behavior. Or you can join a local church youth group, which will most likely include students from your school. You never have to hang out with dangerous or unhealthy people just to have a place to belong.

Watch Your Own Temper

An important part of decreasing your stress comes in learning to control your own potential for violence. That means taking responsibility for your own anger.

In *Overcoming Frustration and Anger,* author P.A. Hauck talks about six steps that often lead us to greater and greater anger:

1. I want something.
2. I didn't get it and I'm frustrated.
3. It's awful and terrible not to get what I want.
4. You shouldn't frustrate me! I must have my way!
5. You are bad for frustrating me.
6. Bad people ought to be punished.[3]

You can see how easy it is to justify violence once we start thinking like this. But God's Word spells out a different way of thinking.

Where do you think all these appalling wars and quarrels come from? Do you think they just happen? Think again.

They come about because you want your own way, and fight for it deep inside yourselves. You lust for what you don't have and are willing to kill to get it. You want what isn't yours and will risk violence to get your hands on it.

You wouldn't think of just asking God for it, would you? And why not? Because you know you'd be asking for what you have no right to. You're spoiled children, each wanting your own way.

You're cheating on God. If all you want is your own way, flirting with the world every chance you get, you end up enemies of God and his way. And do you suppose God doesn't care? The proverb has it that "he's a fiercely jealous lover." And what he gives in love is far better than anything else you'll find. It's common knowledge that "God goes against the willful proud; God gives grace to the willing humble."

So let God work his will in you.

JAMES 4:1-7a, THE MESSAGE

God's Word doesn't say we should stop wanting, it just says that we should take what we want to God and trust him to sort out what's important, what we have no right to, and what would actually harm us. It tells us, in effect, "What he gives in love is far better than anything else you'll find." The sooner you believe that, the sooner you'll be able to deal with your frustrations and angers in a healthy, low-stress way.

STRESSBUSTER:
When you're angry, you need to hear that God is your friend, the one who knows your needs and gets involved.

This is a great time to read from the Book of Psalms. The psalms tell us to "pour out our hearts" to him. We can unload on God, and he will hear. He will not flinch, turn away, scold, mock, or condemn. He will embrace us. He is for us.

What are you angry about right now? Pick up the Book of Psalms and read one, or two, or three of them at random. Before long, you'll find one written by someone who's just as angry as you are—if not more so. Notice that even in their anger, even when it was hard, the psalmists recognized the importance of trusting in God and made a conscious choice to do so.

Help Make School Safe

You may not feel like you have a lot of power, but you can contribute to a school atmosphere where violence is much less likely to happen. Research shows that:

Schools with strong principals; schools that are not too large; schools where discipline is fair, but firm; schools where teachers are imbued with high expectations for every child; schools where parents are drawn into the educational orbit, are schools where learning takes place. They are also schools that are safe.[4]

If your school doesn't have this kind of setup, consider taking action. There is no such thing as being "just a teenager." You *can* make a difference!

STRESSBUSTER:

Here are some ideas of how you can increase the safety of your school:

1. Ask your parents or parent to attend your school's open houses, PTA meetings, and fund-raisers, if they don't do so already. Ask them to meet your teachers and call them about any concerns they have. You may think, "Yeah, right. Like I want my parents down at the school!" But your parents are some of the biggest allies you will ever have.

2. If it seems appropriate, go with your parents to talk to your principal about how academic expectations could be increased. Schools with reasonably high academic expectations increase student self-esteem and are safer. Healthy limits must be observed, however, as academic expectations that are too high bring stresses of their own.

3. With your parents, talk to your school board about backing up your principal concerning work he or she is doing to make your school safer. If violence or racial tension is high, ask your principal to consider starting a teen mediation or peer counseling program in which older students are trained to mediate conflicts between other students. Peer counselors work with a crisis intervention team that includes psychologists, adult counselors, principals, and other school administrators.

4. Consider joining SAVE (Students Against Violence Everywhere). Ask them for additional suggestions on what you can do to take action in your school. Write them at:

   SAVE
   West Charlotte Senior High School
   2219 Senior Drive
   Charlotte, NC 28216

It's easy to feel like school is bigger than you are, and that you are at the mercy of it and its demands. But remember, school is there to help *you*. It's your school.

If you feel like you're drowning in schoolwork, if you feel like you can't keep up with the demands of your friends, if you feel unsafe, take whatever actions you can to help you face your struggles and lower your stress. You have a lot more power to shape your life, including your school life, than you might realize. Make a list of what actions you can take today.

There is no stressbuster quite like finding out you are not helpless. You *can* make a difference.

NINE

Facing Family Stress

Shelley has what appears on the surface to be the perfect life. She is captain of the volleyball team, was voted homecoming queen, is loved by everybody (both in and out of the popular crowd), has a sweet and gorgeous boyfriend, and gets straight A's. But Shelley is miserable.

Why? Because her family is in shambles. Her parents have fought each other for years. And just when it seemed like things couldn't get any worse, they announced that they are going to separate. Shelley is sure they're headed for divorce. With all this stressing her out, how can she enjoy the rest of her life?

Four Family Foundations

When the family is working right, it's obvious that God invented it. It's a place of connection, safety, love, listening, and laughter, where conflicts get resolved in a healthy way. But when the family isn't working, everyone in it becomes miserable.

How do you know if your family is working well—or if it is a source of great stress? You can look at these four foundation stones of a healthy family. The first one is the cornerstone: the most important one, on which the rest of the structure—the family—is built.

1. God is at the center of the family. Parents walk openly and deliberately with Christ and encourage their children to know him.
2. The husband is the head of the home. He is a gentle, firm, sacrificial leader who knows how to establish the direction of the home through discussion with his wife, whom he trusts and whose ideas he respects.
3. The husband and wife have a clearly loving relationship. The kids *know* Dad and Mom care about each other. There's a famous saying: "The greatest thing parents can do for their children is to love each other well."
4. There is a clear distinction between the generations. In other words, parents are in charge and the kids are not. This also means that the kids aren't expected to meet adult needs (like being Mom or Dad's sounding board about their own personal or marital problems). The parents are not permitted to act like children (for example, Dad doesn't spend the college fund money on a new boat because he's having a midlife crisis; Mom doesn't power-shop to soothe her pain).

How does knowing about these foundations work as a stressbuster? It helps you know what God wants for your family, so that if this is not your reality, you can find comfort in knowing you're not crazy for feeling bad about it. Knowing about these four foundations also can help you focus your feelings. A teen might say, "So *that's* why I feel uncomfortable when my dad tells me things I feel like he should only be telling Mom. I'm not supposed to have to meet adult needs!"

Let's keep these four foundations in mind as we look at three common areas of family stress.

Family Malfunction

A lot of people talk about "family dysfunction," but I'm staying away from the word "dysfunction" on purpose. I like using "malfunction" here, because it implies action. Malfunction isn't something that just happens to us. It happens because of choices we make. Families experience pain because they think and do foolish things, and because they neglect one or more of the four foundations.

Donna and Curt's parents haven't gotten along in years. Mom relates mostly to Donna and Curt, while Dad works a lot and reads history books when he's home.

One day, the kids' dad announces that he has a son from a previous marriage that Donna and Curt knew nothing about. The kids are stunned and confused. Later, they find out that their mom knew about their half brother the whole time and resented the time and money her husband spent on him. But she never talked honestly and openly with anyone, including her husband, about her hurt, frustration, and anger. No wonder these parents weren't close! Foundation three was violated for three decades because the painful realities of a first marriage and the existence of an unacknowledged son had never been faced.

Instead of dealing with the pain caused by neglected foundations, families often create *family myths*. These are stories that explain why families "have to" stay stuck where they are. Some examples:

1. Dad is distant from Mom because he works so hard to provide for the family and is so tired by the end of the day.
2. Uncle Henry only drinks a little bit to ease the pain in his legs from the arthritis.
3. Grandma is rigid, cold, and controlling because that's just her personality.
4. Dad gambles because he's a Vietnam veteran, and he should be allowed to deal with his tragic experiences any way that helps him.
5. It's okay that Mom flies into rages, because Dad is hard to live with.
6. The family's behavior patterns come from the misbehavior of my older brother when he was a teenager.[1]

What is the likely truth in each of these cases? (1) Dad is really avoiding intimacy with his wife, because he's afraid he'll be rejected; (2) Uncle Henry doesn't want to quit drinking because he can't face his problems; (3) Grandma is controlling because she is terrified of being powerless; (4) gambling is dangerous—especially when it involves losing money the family needs—and isn't helping Dad to heal; (5) it's never okay to abuse people in your life; and (6) each person is responsible for his or her own behavior.

So what are your options? An effective response would be to start a cycle of honesty rather than dishonesty. In the case of Donna and Curt, both parents told the kids that it was better not to talk about their half brother. At first, the kids did as they were asked. Then they went to their parents, together, and told them: "This is too hard for us. You're putting us through a lot, and we need to be able to talk about this with people we trust. We won't badmouth you, but we have to be able to talk about how we feel."

If their parents continue to forbid the kids to talk about it, they can at least turn to a school counselor, who will give them a safe place to work through their feelings and talk about the way things really are. This allows them to stay in touch with the truth.

You'll be better off learning to tell the truth—good and bad—about your family. You also need to tell yourself the truth about yourself (how you help keep the family myth going).

Family malfunction happens when the four foundations erode. But when a family admits the truth and delves into the pain underneath the myths, those foundations *can* be rebuilt.

Knowing this can defuse your stress, because it gives you hope. It also gives you something constructive to do: you can pray about these foundations, asking God to help strengthen them. As you pray and as you hope, however, remember that your parents are adults. You may (possibly) influence their behavior, but very likely you may not. Your parents may make choices you don't agree with. If this happens, remember, it's not your fault. And God is with you, even when things feel completely out of control. They're really not. He's got you in the palm of his hand.

When Family Malfunction Leads to Divorce

Sometimes, family malfunctions become so bad, the marriage falls apart. People often think that young children suffer the most. But divorce invades a teen's life with as much force as it does a younger child's. It's a mistake to think that teens are immune to divorce's effects.

Adolescents are already in the middle of tons of transitions—from deciding what they believe about God to figuring out who they are and what kind of person they want to be—and they need family stability as much as their younger siblings do. Sometimes, when parents fight a lot, the decision to divorce can come almost as a relief. But with the relief comes big-time grief.

STRESS 101:

Why is divorce so stressful? There are a whole bunch of reasons.

- Single-parent homes are usually under more financial strain than homes in which the marriage stayed intact.
- Kids often think (mistakenly) that the divorce is somehow their fault, and they feel personal failure and guilt.
- Kids often feel torn between their mom and dad, as each parent tries to bring the child over to his or her "side" in various battles.
- Stepparents may come into the picture, and this often multiplies the stress ("Who *is* this person trying to replace my dad or mom?").

STRESSBUSTER:

How do you stressbust in the midst of a divorce? Here are a couple of ideas:

- Keep God at the center. Take your concerns to him in prayer, and turn to his Word for comfort. He doesn't usually wave a magic wand and make things better. (That's because people all have free will, and people, including our parents, are allowed to make their own choices.) But God *does* hear you. He does care. And he is with you, every second of every day—when you're depressed, when you're crying, and when you remember that life still holds a lot of good things for you.

- Remember that God is at the head of both your new homes, whether each of your parents is living alone in an apartment or is remarried. That one important thing has *not* changed.

- Make sure you're willing to let God, not you, be the head of the home you're in. If he's not welcome in your parent's home (this does happen sometimes), you can at least make sure he's the Lord of *your* life.

- Pray for each of them to grow in wisdom and unselfishness. Don't get angry with God if you don't see results right away. These things take time (sometimes a *lot* of time). But God can work in your parents' lives. More importantly, when you pray, he can work in *your* life, making it easier for you to deal with the stress you're under.

- Set healthy boundaries. Resist the temptation to become Mom or Dad's sounding board. Empathize but don't become junior therapist. Urge your parents to find their own friends or counselors and get the help they need.

- Remember that God will care for you, he will not drop you, and he will keep his promises. It's like the hymn says, "Through many dangers, toils, and snares I have already come; 'Tis grace [has] brought me safe thus far, and grace will lead me home." When you're being jerked between two armed camps, know that God will be the safe adult in your life, giving you his grace to lead you home. He hasn't forgotten that you need a home. Even when your own home feels unsafe, you can find a home in him.

- Work out a vision for your own life. There's likely to be little vision for parenting on either side for awhile, but you can create your *own* vision. Do something daring: think outside the box. Decide right now that you're not going to let this divorce ruin your life, or make you an angry, bitter person.

- How do you do this? By believing in God's promises, hoping in God's future for you, and developing goals outside the ones blocked by the divorce. Can't afford Harvard now? Go to a public university. Can't afford the public university? Work your way through. Your parents may be distracted right now, but you can create a vision worth pursuing.

* Let God be the one to step in and parent you. Be willing to be his needy child. He says, "I will be a father to the fatherless." He'll be a mother to the motherless, too. When your parents are struggling and distracted, God will be exactly the parent you need.

Older Kids Caring for Younger Siblings

James really wants to be on the basketball team. But this isn't an option. Every day after school, he has to go home to take care of his little brother, Colin. Both his parents work, and they rely on James to pick up Colin at school and take care of him until six-thirty or seven-thirty.

Each day, there's a list of things James' parents expect of him: (1) make sure Colin does his homework; (2) do his own homework; (3) clean the breakfast dishes; (4) don't go anywhere; (5) don't have friends over; (6) stay off the phone; and (7) start supper. (Lately, "start supper" has come to mean "make dinner all by yourself, because by the time we get home we're all going to be starved.")

Go back to the original four foundations. Which of them is being violated here?

That's right! The only one that's not clearly violated is foundation three: a clearly loving relationship between husband and wife. Foundation one (God at the center) has to be at least somewhat violated, because God's wisdom would show James' parents that they are placing an excessive burden on their son. Foundation two (father as sacrificial leader) has to be violated to a degree, too; because true, unselfish leadership wouldn't allow this shifting the burden onto a child. Foundation four (clear distinction between the generations) is really wiped out in that the teenager is being asked to parent the younger siblings.

Again, don't misunderstand. I'm not saying that a two-income household might not sometimes be necessary. And I firmly agree that teenagers should help out around the house. But when parents expect too much, this can be a real stressor.

In all fairness to James' parents, finding child care for two-income families is tough. They're not the only parents around who have asked an older sibling to act as sort of a surrogate parent. Unfortunately, kids aren't usually asked how they feel about this. Many report that they feel they're coming home to a non-home in the afternoons. This is a recipe for stress—and disaster.

Keep in mind, most teenagers think that their parents ask too much of them. If you feel your parents are requiring too much of you, ask yourself these questions: Am I frustrated because I want more time to spend with my friends? Would I rather hang out in my room than take care of my little brother? Do I feel like I'm not getting enough time to watch TV or play video games?

If these are the worst of your problems, your parents probably aren't asking too much. But if you find that you are feeling extremely stressed out or that you feel like you are one of the responsible adults in the family and that things would fall apart if you weren't in charge, or if you feel increasingly isolated at school because you have no opportunity to connect with other students, then you and your family might have a problem.

Gently but firmly, go to your parents and tell them how you feel. See if together, you can come up with a better arrangement. Is there a relative or a trusted neighbor who could meet you at your home? Does the two-career arrangement have to continue? Do some stressbusting together. You might be surprised at the solutions you find.

A Family You Can Count On

Families can be the biggest creators of stress around. They can also be great stressbusters themselves. No matter what your situation, you're not alone. Every family has its share of difficult siblings, stressed-out parents, broken relationships, and other problems.

The most important thing to remember is, God loves you. He is with you. He won't make the harshest storms disappear, but he will bring you through them. He will bless you for faithfully trying to rebuild your family relationships. And he will continue to be your family, in every way you need him to be: now, and every day for the rest of your life.

TEN

Slaying the Perfectionism Monster

Kate was a good student in junior high. But her mom wanted her to be a *great* student. At the end of her first term in high school, Kate brought home four A's and three B's.

Not good enough, her mom said.

The next term, Kate studied more. Her grades improved: Six A's, one B. Most parents would be thrilled. Kate's mom expressed only disappointment.

These days, Kate does nothing but study. She's determined to get straight A's—for the rest of her high school career. Nothing else will do. She can't bear to disappoint her mom again.

What Kate doesn't realize is that her mom is facing her own bad memories. She wishes she'd had enough money to go to college, and she's worried she can't afford to send Kate. Desperate to solve the problem, she's put the entire burden on Kate's shoulders, hoping Kate will win a scholarship. Kate doesn't know what's going on. She only knows that she's not measuring up. And the stress is killing her.

"Be Perfect—or At Least Have the Decency to Pretend You Are."

Why do teens want so badly to perform perfectly? Because somehow, they've gotten the message that that's what's required for them to be acceptable. It's not enough just to do a good job at something—many teens feel pressure to perform flawlessly at *everything.*

STRESSBUSTER:
Get out a piece of paper. Write down every source of the message, "Be perfect!" you can think of. Use the list below for help (remember, you don't have to come up with a perfect list!):

- TV (both ads and shows feature thin people without flaws)
- magazines (look at the covers and say no more)
- parents (sometimes their anxieties push us to succeed more than is healthy)
- the mall (gotta have the right stuff, or you'll be a *loser*)
- the mail (five colleges a day want you, but you have to be *great* to get in)
- some varieties of Christianity

Now, put down the book and go make your own list. The book is very obedient and will wait right here for you.

Okay, what did you come up with? Are you surprised at how many perfectionistic messages you're getting?

In a classic book on parenting, author David Elkind introduces the idea of the "hurried child"—that is, the child who is pushed to achieve, measure up, get ready for reading, even make the country proud by coming in ahead of Chinese students in math scores. The research of Elkind and other experts has produced the term, "the superkid syndrome." According to author and education specialist Judy Loken, a superkid is indeed hurried along: "... hurried to babysitters, hurried to piano lessons, hurried to gymnastics, hurried to soccer, hurried to dance lessons, hurried to achieve, hurried to grow up."[1]

Do you feel like a hurried teen? Do you feel pressure to be a "superkid"? Today's society says, "Woe to the child who develops on schedule" (rather than ahead of time), and "Super-woe to the late bloomer." The message from many parents, schools, and media is "Hurry up and be perfect yesterday, or become a permanent loser." Teens hear, "Get to work!" and that's just what a lot of them do. Teacher and writer Miriam Adderholdt-Elliott offers the following insight.

Children between ages 6 and 12 are at risk for becoming workaholics if they are rewarded for the things they *do* rather than for the personal qualities they have and are developing. In other words, the child who is praised for bringing home perfect papers but not for being a nice person, having a sense of humor, being playful, taking risks, showing kindness and gentleness, and being a good friend is likely to think that work is the most important part of life. The child gets "hooked" on working hard because he or she knows that it will bring rewards.[2]

Kids who measure themselves through work and accomplishments are in danger of becoming perfectionists. A perfectionist is someone who can't relax until he or she has met the highest possible standard. Anything less is seen as failure. This means a perfectionist almost never relaxes. The perfectionist's mind works something like this: *There's success (which is meeting the highest standard), and then there are the following degrees of failure: "failure, big failure, huge failure, enormous failure, gargantuan failure."* [3] The perfectionist thinks in this all-or-nothing pattern: you either hit a home run or you're laughed out of the ballpark.

Perfectionism and Eating Disorders

Reaching for perfection is super stressful. Even when you reach your goals, there's always a new range of mountains to climb. Sixteen-year-old Melanie put it this way, "When I bring home all A's on my report card, there's a celebration *that day*. The next day, the message is, 'Back to the grind. There's another report card coming up in nine weeks.'"

I asked Melanie, "Where does that message come from?"

"It's from my parents, for sure," she answered. "But it's also from me."

"Okay," I said, "let's start with the part that comes from your parents. How do you feel when they imply it's time to get back to work?"

Melanie thought for a moment, then answered, "I feel a little angry. Then I feel like, 'Yeah, it's time to get back to work.

I don't want to blow it the next nine weeks.'"

Melanie's mixed feelings contain a seed of anger that could very well build into rage. The rage comes from the hurt in her heart that's trying to say, "Can't anyone see I want time to relax, to play, to stare at the ceiling, to refuel? I'm exhausted, and I'm only sixteen. I have no control over my life."

If Melanie doesn't do some stressbusting pretty soon, here's what could happen. Her rage and helplessness could build until her need for control triggers a search for a way to gain control *that no one else can stop.*

Teens who share Melanie's struggle often wind up using food as the method for exerting control. After all, unless someone force-feeds her (an extremely unpleasant task), no one can make her eat an ounce more than she wants. Anorexia often begins because a person wants to rebel against perfectionism (and rightly so). It is a bad and dangerous solution, however, and it must be treated by medical professionals as soon as it's detected. Thankfully, the energy that fuels it can be redirected and channeled toward a positive, healthy war against the inner and outer pressures to be perfect. Underneath, anorexia is a cry for freedom. Thankfully, the person who wants to escape the need for perfection can find freedom in other ways.

Bulimics also wage a battle against perfectionism. But while the anorexic sees food as control, the bulimic sees it as a form of comfort. The message "be perfect" brings pressure, strain, tension, and burden. The perfectionist carries a weight of instructions on her shoulders (instructions about what to do, how to do it, and when). Bending low under this load, she longs for kind words, a peaceful hour or two, a helping hand, permission to rest. Then she notices that certain foods create a feeling of warmth and comfort. The illusion that she is being cared for grows along with the food intake.

Unfortunately, in her mind she still has to be perfect, and getting fat is a *major* no-no. What to do? The first time she throws up, she's disgusted; but then she likes the feeling of emptiness it brings. It doesn't take long to learn to tolerate the unpleasantness of barfing, because the payoff of continued thinness seems so powerful. What the person suffering from bulimia doesn't know is, such false power can kill her.

Stressbusting Perfectionism by Finding Grace

Before we jump into this section, note that we're stressbusting perfectionism, not anorexia or bulimia. If you're struggling with these eating disorders, *get help.* Call the American Association of Christian Counselors (1-800-526-8673) to find someone who can help you, or turn to a trusted counselor, youth pastor, teacher, or relative.

Wow, you may be wondering. *Is trying to be perfect so bad?*

In a word: yes. Why? Because that's not what God wants from you, or from anyone else.

In fact, the Bible takes a major stand against perfectionism. Verse after verse makes it clear: God alone is perfect. No one compares to him. Perfectionists are trying to attain the unattainable. In a way, they're trying to be God. For another thing, the Bible is overflowing with the message of God's grace.

What is grace? In a nutshell, grace is *undeserved favor.* Grace emphasizes God's kindness and the liberty with which he offers it.[4] Jesus is God's grace in the form of a Person who died for us, setting us free from sin, guilt, death, and hell. On the basis of these freedoms, he frees us from the pressure to be perfect. Jesus is the sun of grace coming up and warming our hearts, inviting us to play, sing, party, celebrate, give thanks, worship. This is far from the grim duty to be perfect!

The only one who is perfect in this world is Jesus. Do we deserve his grace? *No,* and that's the joy of it. It's a gift, pure and simple. When we're trying to be perfect, we're afraid of being judged. We figure perfection will protect us from any criticism (judgment) the world could bring on us. But Christ has taken all judgment out of our future by pronouncing a positive judgment on us *now.* God *does* judge us—but positively! He says, "You pass with flying colors! Now, come sit on my lap and let's begin that close, loving relationship that starts now and lasts forever."[5] This is grace.

Because grace is real, we don't have to be perfect. God loves us as falling-short sinners. He calls us to come to him in trust and to learn obedience. But the "measuring up" we need will never come from our performance; it will always come from Christ who "measures up" for us.

Now, when we fall short—when we blow a test, mouth off to our parents, lie to a friend, compromise our purity, or make any other poor choice—we can look at it and learn from it instead of hiding it. We can, as Henry Cloud says, learn to integrate the good and the bad in us.[6] Instead of hiding the bad in shame, we can bring it to God in confession and prayer. At the cross we can face it, knowing we are secure in God's love.

God loves you like you've always wanted to be loved. You don't have to be perfect, because you're already spoken for. God himself has spoken for you.

What could be more perfect than that?

ELEVEN

Defending Your Beliefs

L ast week in youth group, Darren learned that the Bible tells Christians to "witness" to others—that is, to share the good news of what Jesus did for us in dying for our sins, rising from the dead, and offering us forgiveness.

Darren has never witnessed before, and he doesn't know where to begin. So he grabs a handful of tracts—small paper booklets that help Christians tell others about Christ—and takes them to school on Monday.

In the lunchroom, he corners his friend Brad, who has already told Darren he doesn't believe in God—and doesn't want to.

"Hey, Brad. Come here. I have something I need to tell you."

"Sure man, what's up?"

Sweating, Darren opens up his tract. "Did you know that you're a sinner?"

"*What?*"

Darren nervously flips through the booklet. He has started on the wrong page. "I mean ... do you have a relationship with God?"

"Do I *what?*" This conversation has come from out of the blue. Brad is looking at Darren like he's crazy.

After a few more minutes of sweating and stuttering,

Darren crumples the tract up and crams it in his pocket. "Never mind," he mutters, vowing never to try witnessing again. "Forget I said anything."

"Sure." Brad shakes his head. "Whatever."

As you just saw, Brad really didn't want to hear what Darren had to say. Especially not then.

It's hard for us as Christians to know how to share our Christian beliefs with others. It's also stressful to go to school and live out those beliefs when the people around us are, at best, barely tolerant—at worst, hostile—toward our faith.

When you want respect from the people around you and they disrespect—or just don't care about—your faith, it's tempting to respond by shutting up about Jesus. We all want to be liked, and to be known for loving and accepting people; at the same time, we want our friends to know about the Jesus we love, and who loves us. This creates a huge conflict within us. It's a drag. It feels bad. It's *stressful*.

So what can we do about it?

Learning to Speak Up About Christ

Darren meant well. But he was going about the thing all wrong. As you probably know, people won't listen to Christians when they think we're spouting robotic lines we've learned off a three-by-five card. They want us to speak from our hearts, not from a stale memory job. It's not that using memorized material is wrong, but generally people want our hearts involved first.

A less planned-out, but more heartfelt presentation of the gospel would have had a much better chance of catching Brad's attention—and heart. "Canned" gospel tastes about as good as canned green beans. What would taste better? Something fresh, of course! What could be more fresh than an honest story from your heart about how Christ has changed you or how he is working in your life?

Chances are, you've seen the movie *Titanic*—maybe even a dozen times!—and you probably think you know the story at least pretty well. But what got left out of the film (because Leonardo diCaprio's character, Jack, had to have more time to dally with Rose, played by Kate Winslet) was the incredible, real-life effort made by another ship, the *Carpathia,* to rescue the *Titanic.* Here is a passage from the book *"Unsinkable": The Full Story of the RMS Titanic:*

At the *Carpathia's* top speed of fourteen knots she would cover the distance between herself and the *Titanic* in four hours, which was not good enough for [Captain] Rostron. Now he swung into action.

Returning to the chartroom he called for Chief Engineer Johnstone. Speed, he told Johnstone, he wanted more speed than the old *Carpathia* had ever mustered. Call out the off-duty watch to the engine room, get every available stoker roused to feed the furnaces. Cut off the heat and hot water to passenger and crew accommodations, put every ounce of steam the boilers made into the engines....

Down in the boiler room the extra hands were put to

work shoveling coal into the furnaces of the boilers. First the safety valves were closed off, then the engineers began to systematically shut off steam to the rest of the ship, ducting it instead into the ... engines. Up, down, up, down, up, down, the pistons pounded, as the chief engineer watched the revolutions steadily increasing. Faster and faster the ship drove ahead—14 knots ... 14 1/2 ... 15 ... 16 ... 16 1/2 ... 17 knots. The old *Carpathia* had never gone so fast....

Hoping to give some hope to those aboard the sinking ship, Rostron began firing colored rockets, interspersed with Cunard Roman candles, every fifteen minutes. Down below the stokers and firemen shoveled coal like they never had before and every plate and rivet in the ship shook with the exertion as the *Carpathia* thundered on. As one crewman later quipped, "The old boat was as excited as any of us."

The *Carpathia* was steaming hard from the south.... Soon the ship's green sidelight could be seen as the vessel loomed over the horizon, still firing rockets, still coming hard.[1]

When I read about Captain Rostron's passion for the sufferers aboard the *Titanic,* I want to cry and cheer. In Rostron's furious rush to get to the *Titanic* I see the Lord's passion and resolution as he comes hard for me in spite of the devil, sin, hell, death, and chaos. He comes for me, crashing through every obstacle this world can hurl into his path. How God got me in his loving grip—*that* is a story I want to tell. Our personal life stories, like the *Titanic,* provide a stirring picture of God as he pulls out all the stops and stops at nothing to save us.

Have you experienced God's forgiveness after cheating on a test? Has he helped you mend a broken friendship? Do you find comfort in knowing that he's there for you, no matter what you do or say? That's the story your friends need to hear. That's the truth they need to know. You don't need to worry about saying "the right thing." Just say what's true.

Your friends at school can connect with the idea of feeling lost, and of needing someone to be with them during the tough times. Many have been left by friends seeking greater popularity. Some have been forsaken by parents who pursued their own desires, at the expense of their families. Some feel as though they've abandoned themselves: they are mad at themselves for choices they've made and don't know where to go for mercy. You can tell them where to find forgiveness and grace. It doesn't have to be hard. Just speak from the heart.

When we demonstrate the gospel in this way, others begin to wonder about God—just as the survivors of the *Titanic* wondered about the *Carpathia*—"Will he come to save me, too?"

He will. That's all they need to know. That's all you need to say. God will take care of the rest.

No stress.

TWELVE

Struggling Against Sexual Stress

Seventeen-year-old Jamie is experiencing one of the hardest years of her life. Her parents are divorcing, her little brother is undergoing treatment for leukemia, and between worrying and taking time off from school to help her mother, Jamie is barely passing her classes—and it's her senior year!

Jamie's parents are so preoccupied with their son's illness, they've had little time to devote to Jamie. So when a cute guy at school asks her out, Jamie is thrilled with the attention— even after he starts kissing her passionately and pushing her to go further than she knows she should. She knows she's not *supposed* to have sex with him. But she really wants to. She can't help it. She loves the attention. She loves how good it feels to be held by someone. Nothing else is going right in her life. Why shouldn't she be allowed to have this?

Sex: The Answer That's Not an Answer

Jamie thinks that having sex with Wes will make her feel better. What she doesn't know is this: Trying to meet your needs through premarital sex is like trying to beat eggs with a chain saw. Why? Like sex, a chain saw is a heavy burden and extremely hard to control. For another, those who use it can get really hurt.

Jamie is lonely. You might be, too. Now, more than ever, you need to know that sex is *never* the right tool for getting your emotional needs met. Sex seems like an act of the body, but it's really an act of the soul.

It is a common belief that sex can feel good at the time and leave no lasting effects. This is just not true. Sex unites two souls in a way nothing else can. Once you've connected sexually, there's no way to go your separate ways—tomorrow, next year, or after graduation—without doing serious damage to your soul and spirit. Unless you're married when you have sex, you are taking a terrible, terrible risk—in more ways than one.

STRESSBUSTER:

Sometimes teens succumb to sexual temptation because they are so desperate for physical affection. No wonder! Physical touch is a tremendous stress reliever.

Make sure you're getting enough pure, appropriate physical touch in your life. Author Barbara Johnson writes, "A hug can relieve tension, improve blood flow, reduce stress, boost self-esteem, and generate goodwill. Hugs cure a lot more than whatever ails you. They keep you immune to illness of the mind."* So hug your parents, siblings, grandparents and friends. You'll help relieve their stress, too!

* Barbara Johnson, *The Best Devotions of Barbara Johnson*
(Grand Rapids, Mich.: Zondervan, 2001), 185.

The Sex-for-Love Trap

Premarital sex devastates millions of young people every year. You would think that, after the sexually-transmitted disease epidemic, the AIDS epidemic, the proliferation of teen pregnancy, and the emotional toll taken in millions of lives, sex outside of marriage would be seen for what it is: an attack on the human heart. But we as a society are still learning. Here is a list of the heart issues involved in every sexual encounter:

- the issue of anonymity—Am I just a body that's at the right place and time? Am I treating my partner that way?
- the issue of dignity—Am I just being used? Am I using my partner?
- the issue of truth—Was I lied to, so that I would agree to have sex? Or, have I lied to get what I want sexually?
- the issue of integrity—Do my values dictate my behavior, or do I drop them when I want something else?
- the issue of love—Is it possible to love unconditionally or does love always involve giving something in order to *get* something else?
- the issue of trust—Can I trust my partner to care or am I just a means to an end? Am *I* trustworthy?
- the issue of respect—Can I get attention without trading sex for it? Am I willing to lose my partner's favor if I won't give myself away sexually? Can having sex ever bring me real respect, or does it *cost* me respect in the end?
- the issue of self-concept—How am I going to look at myself in the long run if I give myself away sexually? Or,

do I have to get others to give themselves to me sexually for me to feel good about myself?

This list has a message: Sex is never just sex; it's always tied to deep issues of the heart. The sexual revolution (which began in the late sixties of the last century and continues in various forms today) said that casual sex is fine if both parties consent. But consent has to be *informed* for it to be real, and it's *not informed*. In other words, as a culture, we don't really know what we're doing!

Years ago, the Bible played a much greater role in informing the views of our society about what was right and wrong. Sadly, today, our culture largely ignores the Bible's teachings, particularly when they are in conflict with the way people *want* to be allowed to live.

Two or three hundred years ago, however, people would have thought it strange to consider sex outside of marriage an option, much less morally *right*. They'd have known that extramarital sex mixes something holy (sex) with something unholy (the lack of a covenant, or lasting, unbreakable promise), something that never works.

Why doesn't it work? Because real love takes time. God has good reasons for wanting us to have sex only within the covenant of marriage. He knows it takes time to create a trustworthy, reliable unity between unrelated persons. It's hard enough for those related by blood to stay faithful to each other. It's even harder for those related only by love. Since unconditional love has to be learned, and since learning it takes time, a covenant (sealed in their marriage vows) binds two people together, giving them time to work out the details of loving one another. That covenant strengthens them after the time their initial love (which is pretty much looking out for itself) loses power. During that time, they learn to love unconditionally so that when "the honeymoon is over," they know how to choose love, even when they don't feel it.

It's impossible to learn that outside of marriage. And dabbling in sexual activity outside of these bounds can only bring you heartache.

Pregnancy: One of the Biggest Stressors of All

Earlier, we touched briefly upon the dangers of pregnancy. But it's so common and potentially so devastating, it bears more discussion.

Everywhere you turn, people are talking about the pleasures of easy sex, but almost everyone is in denial about the possibility that sex may end in conception. (A strange thing not to consider, since that's one thing sex is meant to do.)

As you consider the dangers of sexual activity, you need to know this: the only surefire way to prevent a crisis pregnancy is to remain abstinent until marriage. Sexual abstinence is one of the most powerful stressbusters of all. A baby is *not* a baby doll, and getting pregnant before marriage is *not* like playing house. The stresses of crisis pregnancy are many, because a tiny, needy child lands in the middle of an unprepared person's life. The results are difficult, painful, and overwhelming.

Because of this reality, many young women opt to "solve" their pregnancy problems through abortion. In the short run, abortion seems to make the problem disappear. This is not true, however. In fact, abortion only replaces a crisis pregnancy with many, more devastating, and even longer-lasting problems: crippling guilt, shame, and heartache.

You can save yourself from all these kinds of suffering simply by following God's rules for sexual purity. I know of some teens who have stressed out about not having dates. (This is a problem that generally solves itself in time.) But no one ever stressed out about being too sexually pure.

STRESSBUSTER:

Have you already lost your virginity? Are you pregnant? Don't panic. This wasn't God's original plan for you, but it's not the end of the world. As you know, there are a lot of problems that come with sexual activity. But it's never too late to get back on the right path. You're not ruined. God loves you every bit as much as he always did.

Take your worries and your guilt to God in prayer. Consider taking your concerns to a caring parent, your youth pastor, or a Crisis Pregnancy Center worker. (These folks are trained to help young people face sexual crises, even if they're not pregnant.)

It is never too late to make a fresh start.

Want to do some serious stressbusting in your life? It's simple: Save yourself for marriage, and for the one person— your spouse—who will have the God-given right to love you in that way. You'll never regret it.

And you'll avoid a whole lot of big-time stress along the way.

THIRTEEN

Juggling Priorities

Joshua had a plan for his sophomore year. This was the year he was going to live the kind of life he really wanted. He wanted to get better grades, find the time to play on the soccer team, and spend more time with his friends. That meant that he would have to quit his part-time job at the gas station and probably stop driving his car (since he wouldn't be able to afford the gas and insurance). But he was tired of living such a hectic life. He was still in high school, and he wanted time to enjoy it.

When the school year started, however, Josh realized that he would have to work a few more weeks if he was going to get the stereo he wanted for his car. Then, once he had the stereo installed, the idea of parking the Volkswagen Jetta for the school year seemed ridiculous. Before long, Josh found himself working more than ever, even while he was trying to study, hang out with his friends, and play soccer.

Priorities are like dental hygiene: everybody thinks tooth care is a good idea, but how many people floss regularly? The same thing is true of priorities: we all think we should put the things we really care about first in our lives, but we get overwhelmed by daily life and our priorities just don't get the attention we intend them to.

If establishing priorities is such a good idea, why is it so hard to do? Why does our life so often decide what we do, instead of the other way around?

STRESSBUSTER:
Homework can be one of the biggest stressors in a teen's life. Often it's one of the last things we want to do, so we put it off until it's almost too late. You don't have to beat yourself up if that's the way you usually do things. But you *can* make things easier for yourself.

Create a "to do" list and put your assignments on it. Give yourself several "due dates" for big assignments: one for a first draft and a second and possibly a third for later drafts. It's tempting to wait until a paper is almost due before starting it. But by getting it out of the way, you'll relieve a lot of stress—and make life a lot more enjoyable for yourself! The same rule applies to smaller class assignments, and to your chores at home. Try it. You'll be surprised at the results!

So Many Voices, So Little Time

There are millions of voices out there, calling out to get your and your friends' attention. Don't believe it? Thumb through any mass-media teen magazine and consider the wide range of often conflicting messages it has for you.

One recent issue promised an article entitled "Let's Talk About Sex" (the most over-talked subject in the universe but still guaranteed to draw readers), while another considered the benefits of abstinence. Another article talked about the "secret" life of the latest blonde, skinny, sexy celebrity female dancer/vocalist of the month (it turns out she likes peach and vanilla yogurt swirled together—whoa!), while another urged readers to like themselves just as they are (skinny, blonde celebrity or not). Another article featured "things girls never tell guys" (but girls will tell a magazine that's aimed at telling everybody!).

These voices (and countless others) yell advice at teens: "Be this! Don't do that! Wear those! Don't go here! Do go there! Use (fill-in-the-blank) makeup—or be a loser! Shop here! Get! Use! Get some more! *Use* some more! Avoid this product! Buy this one, no matter what!" The voices never stop.

Have you ever noticed that the hosts of teen shows on TV are often yelling? They sound like used car salesmen, only smoother. Their voices are designed to jerk you awake and grab you long enough to deliver you over to the advertisers. (Did you know that one major purpose of TV is to supply a passive, entertained audience to advertisers?)

This blizzard of opinions and orders has a huge impact on your priorities—or lack of them. *Priorities* are about what's to come *prior,* or first, in your life. Scripture says, "seek *first* his kingdom and his righteousness, and all these things will be given to you as well" (Matthew 6:33, NIV, italics mine).

How do we do this? Let's take a look.

Identify the Influences Around You

Magazines and TV aren't just forms of entertainment; they are master manipulators designed to shape your opinions, and they are at work on *you.*

The manipulators behind entertainment are incredibly skilled at lowering your defenses and delivering the worldview *they* want you to have while they deliver *you* to—you guessed it—the advertisers. They don't tell you they're going to do this, so they're dishonest on top of everything else. Would you let any *person* do this to you? Why would you allow an entertainment empire to do it?

Once you recognize what's happening, you can decide what to do about it.

Find Your Passion

Do you want to find out what you care about most? Look to your priorities. You won't have to look far to find the passion underneath. Here, "passion" means whatever you feel strongly about and will go to some trouble to do. Others can tell you what your priorities *should* be, but if you don't feel passion about the suggested priorities, you won't do them for very long or not at all.

When Jesus says, "Seek first God's kingdom and his righteousness," he's assuming you have a passion for God. But, you might ask, "How can Jesus assume that? Sometimes I just don't know how I feel about God. In fact, I do know that I don't *always* feel passionate about him."

Fair enough. So let's look at this further. Jesus seems to think that the more you know God, the more passionately you will love him. Remember, Jesus was a preacher, among other things. When he spoke these words, he was in the middle of an incredibly powerful speech we know as "The Sermon on the Mount." Here's what he said:

Do not store up for yourselves treasures on earth, where moth and rust destroy, and where thieves break in and steal. But store up for yourselves treasures in heaven, where moth and rust do not destroy, and where thieves do not break in and steal.

MATTHEW 6:19-20, NIV

Notice that *Jesus is concerned that you have treasure.* He knows that you want to be satisfied in your life, that you want to be happy, so he proposes that you go after treasure with all your heart. Only, he says, go after the treasure that will never fail you.

What kind of treasure is that? Jesus talks about two kinds of treasure. First, there's the treasure of earthly things, status, power, and privilege. He says these treasures will fail you; they will break your heart. They'll disappoint you, either because they grow weaker in their ability to satisfy, or because others will steal them. Later, Jesus says, "Where your treasure is, there your heart will be also" (Matthew 6:21, NIV). What you treasure will capture your heart; then, when it rusts away or is stolen, the loss will break your heart.

Jesus doesn't want this to happen to you! He says, in essence, "No! Don't go toward earthly treasure. Instead, let me tell you about a treasure that connects you with heaven. Nothing can take these treasures away from you! Store them up! Go wild!"

This second type of treasure Jesus talks about is the kind we will learn about completely only after we die and are with the Lord forever in eternal life. Those treasures are described in 1 Corinthians 3:14 (NIV): "If what [a man] has built survives, he will receive his reward." The writer isn't talking about the reward of salvation but rewards *beyond* salvation. Whatever these treasures are, Jesus has already said they *can't* be taken from you.

Again, Jesus is passionate that this not happen. Why should you be passionate about God? Because he is incredibly passionate about you! He wants to take care of you! He loves you beyond your wildest dreams. He loves you so much, he won't let you use his love for your own aims. Instead, he loves you as he sees fit, provides for your immediate needs, and takes you deeper to provide for the needs you don't yet know you have. You say you can't feel that love? Be patient. Don't worry about feeling it yet. Start with *imagining* it.

Develop Your Spiritual Imagination

Developing a spiritual imagination might sound like odd advice, but it's actually essential to a strong, healthy Christian life. Why do you think the Bible uses so many word pictures and metaphors, and so much poetry? Because these approaches stir our imagination and help us to understand better how much God loves us.

What do you imagine when you read Scripture? Do you read it as though it's a tired textbook? Or, do you read it as what it is: a fire built to melt your frozen heart? As you read it, your imagination can form pictures filled with hope and courage, and these pictures in turn can help you draw closer to God.

Here's a passage in a novel by Milan Kundera that illustrates the heart's true relationship with Christ.

[H]er soul would rise to the surface of her body like a crew charging up from the bowels of a ship, spreading out over the deck, waving at the sky and singing in jubilation.[1]

When our hearts glimpse Christ through our awakened imaginations—when we picture him as lion, shepherd, warrior, brother, slain lamb, king, bright morning star, prophet, priest, master, saving help, and so on—our hearts rise to the surface like this crew charging up from inside the ship. Imagine that crew: they've been confined below decks for days, starving for sunlight. Finally, they are let loose, and they pound up the steps, spread out over the deck, and sing and dance under the blessed sun. *Our* hearts want to sing and dance under the Blessed Son.

Jana had a hard time picturing God's love for her. She knew it in her head, but somehow it just didn't feel real.

One day, after her ballet class, Jana was waiting for her mom to pick her up, and she was picturing herself dancing alone across the floor. Suddenly, in her mind, she imagined God stepping into the room, taking her in his arms, and whirling her around the room. Did this actually, physically happen? No. But this picture gave Jana the clearest picture she'd ever had of God's love for her. He loved her enough to step into her dance class and dance with her. Imagination or not, it was a representation of real truth—God's tender, fatherly love for Jana—and that picture changed her life.

Do you see how imagination leads to love and worship of God? Do you see how worship shows us a God who is passionate toward us? Our old priorities lose their power as we stoke these new passions for God. As we order our passions and redirect them toward God through healthy, receptive spiritual imaginations, our feelings will follow. So will our priorities.

Learn the Difference Between Passion and Intensity

Passion is caring about eternal things. Intensity means caring about the temporary—the things that won't last but only pretend to last (like fame or monetary wealth). Since passion has a foundation that lasts forever, it burns steadily. Intensity first imitates through a false enthusiasm and a seemingly solid determination, but quickly burns out.

The "treasures" you see promoted loudly by the media represent intensity, not passion. Don't be fooled. TV, magazines, radio, etc., have to overdo it to keep you from noticing the emptiness under the glitz and glitter, so they resort to intensity. But intensity doesn't make your soul want to rise up, like the ship's crew, to dance on the deck. Only passion can do that, because passion is a hope-filled, heart-leaping answer to God's enthusiastic pursuit of us.

Letting God Establish Your Priorities

You've noticed, I'm sure, this chapter isn't about coming up with a list of strategies to be more organized, or to put your list of things to do into some kind of order. It's about understanding what you care about most, and letting that passion seep into every nook and cranny of your life.

There are influences in this world that will try to distract you. And sometimes, they'll succeed. But as you draw closer to God, and as you listen more and more to his voice and dive into his Word, his priorities will shape *your* priorities. This will not only ease your stress, it will bring you closer than ever to him.

I can't think of anything more important than that. Can you?

FOURTEEN

Coping With Troubled Friends

It's the third call of the night from Sally to Christine, and this call is not much different than the first two. Sally is feeling depressed, and she's looking to Christine for reassurance.

"Is there something wrong with me?" Sally asks. "Why don't I have more friends?" Basically, Sally is asking, "Am I a worthwhile person?" Christine has said "yes" to this question in every way possible over the three years they've known each other. But she's getting tired. She doesn't know what else to say. She racks her brain, trying to find a way to put it differently—hoping against hope that the message will sink in this time.

If Sally calls me again tonight, Christine thinks, *I will scream.* But she feels guilty about even thinking this, because Sally has made references to suicide in the past. Christine is sort of glad Sally trusts her enough to talk to her. It's just more stress than she can handle to have the weight of Sally's life and happiness on her shoulders.

To Rescue Is to Ruin

In an earlier chapter, I used the story of the *Titanic* and *Carpathia* to illustrate how God moves passionately toward us, to save us. When God does the rescuing, it's a good thing. But in this chapter, we'll look at rescue in a different light. When you or I are asked to do the rescuing instead of God, rescue becomes a bad thing. When we rescue, we intend to help someone, but actually we cause harm by doing something for them that he or she could do alone.

Recently, I had this conversation with a teen I'll call Bob.

BOB: My dad came home drunk again the other night.

ME: How do you know he was drunk?

BOB: I found him in the hall. He'd fallen down, was still passed out, and had gotten sick.

ME: What happened then?

BOB: I dragged him to bed.

ME: Why didn't you leave him right there?

BOB: He's my dad! I couldn't leave him there in that mess.

ME: I see. So what did he learn when he woke up in a warm bed?

BOB (thinking about this a moment): What? Oh, I see. Well ... I guess he learned that he can get drunk, drive home and put others' lives at risk, then wake up in a nice bed.

ME: And what do you think that teaches him?

BOB (starting to get it): Not only that there are no consequences for his actions, but that he's actually rewarded by waking up safe and warm, with everything taken care of for him. Maybe that wasn't the best idea. Is that what you're saying?

How do you respond to this dialogue? Do you lean on the side of "compassion"? If you were Bob and you had his dad, would you want to make sure he got to bed? Or, do you come down on the side of "toughness"? Would you rather see him left where he is, in order for him to learn?

I have two thoughts about this: One, the second approach is certainly more compassionate than the first, because it doesn't reinforce drunkenness; and two, either way, learning takes place: it's just a matter of what he's learning. Getting Bob's dad to bed teaches him to drink without consequences. Letting him lie in his mess teaches him that drinking can lead to painful humiliation.

Maybe it's clearer now what I mean when I say, "to rescue is to ruin." Rescue ruins others because:

- it gets them used to being dependent on others.
- it robs them of chances to build their own "muscles" for facing life.
- it tells them (untruthfully) that they don't have what it takes to handle life without constant help.

Not only does rescuing keep people from learning important lessons but, after awhile, the rescued person becomes a passive complainer, always trying to get others to do what the complainer could do for him- or herself.

Paul's dad continually drank himself to sleep, even though he was supposed to be watching his kids while his wife was at work. When his wife complained about it, he said, "If you'd keep this house cleaner, maybe I'd think about not drinking as much. It's so cluttered around here, it's depressing." What did Paul's mom do? She began staying up late at night, cleaning the house!

What do you think happened? That's right. Her husband kept drinking just as much. By the time she figured out that her response wasn't working, six wasted months had gone by. She was doing the rescuing, and he was ruining himself.

Here's another rescue story. Perhaps you know someone like this. Jennifer is dating a guy who dropped out of high school. He lost his license because of several DUIs, so he expects her to skip school several times a week and drive him around. Her grades are going down, and the guy is still drinking.

When her friends ask her why she puts up with this, she says, "Because he loves me." Jennifer is in serious trouble. What do you think? Would real love impose on the loved one so much that her grades get wrecked? Would real love not care about whether she gets into the college she's always dreamed of attending? He doesn't love her; he finds her pleasant and convenient. She's useful to him in the same way that a sleeping bag or a can opener would be on a camping trip.

How Can You Recognize Someone Who Wants to Be Rescued?

Sometimes, people just want rescue and are not looking for real help. Here are some clues to help you identify these folks.

You Start Feeling Crazier and Angrier

When someone seeks rescue, you start to feel as though this needy person is sucking the life out of you. He doesn't respect your schedule, so you find yourself waiting an hour for him to show up. When he does finally show, he attempts to defuse your anger by saying, "My dad was all over my case, so I had to do what he wanted. I tried to call, but you'd already left." If this happens once, or maybe even twice, it might be true. But if it's a pattern, watch out! You've got a rescue victim on your hands.

You're Providing More and More Special Treatment

When you start rescuing a person, you do things for him you wouldn't do for anyone else. "If you don't pick me up at work and get me over to my friend's house, I won't get to play in his band," he says. When you pick him up, he offers to pay for gas. Then he never does. Pretty soon, you're driving him wherever he wants to go.

Underneath this pattern is the fact that the needy person has a high sense of entitlement. That is, he feels the world owes him big time. And the world has sent *you* to do the paying. Red alert! It's time to back off and stop rescuing. He can find his own way around town (or do his own homework, or find out what people think of him, or whatever else he's asking) without you. The kindest thing you can do is say "No."

You Get Blamed for Things That Aren't Your Fault

The needy person has a sharp sense of when to pass on the blame, and the buck *never* stops with him. Somehow, it's somebody else's fault.

He might say to his date, "Could you pay for the movie? My brother won my date money in a poker game last night. I promise I'll pay you back." Or, he may "forget" to do an errand he promised to do for you when you loaned him your car because "your clunky car was so loud, I couldn't think." Somehow, he managed to do the things *he* wanted to do on his little excursion. You're just out of luck.

This, too, is the mark of someone who is manipulating you into performing a rescue.

You Find Yourself in Chaos More and More Often

Needy people thrive on chaos. Negative energy fuels them, so they like to stir things up. Chaos shoots them full of adrenaline. A needy person may come up to you at a high school football game and tell you that a close friend of yours "is really mad at you." You ask why. "I'm not supposed to tell," he answers, "but I think it's because you didn't give her a ride to the game."

You don't remember offering anyone a ride. If you're not careful, you're going to end up withdrawing from the one who's supposedly mad at you (which is what the needy person wants, so he can have you all to himself—all the more of you to rescue him with!).[1]

Needy People Are After Drama, Not Growth

To people who crave rescue, life is a soap opera and they play the starring victim-role. Deep down, they feel the only way they can get attention is to be needy and lost. God has so much more for them, and if you rescue them over and over, they'll just take that much longer to find out what God is up to in their lives. You'll do a lot more good if, like a mother bird, you gently push them out of the nest and force them to fly on their own.

What Does It Mean to Give Real Help?

We've talked about how to recognize people who need rescuing, and we've explored the reasons why it's not good for you to give them the rescue they want. But isn't that selfish? Doesn't God want us to help others? Isn't that what living out the gospel is all about?

That's right. But God wants us to give *real* help that strengthens people, not false help that weakens them. Here are some examples.

Real Help Speaks the Truth in Love

Ephesians 4:15 (NASB) tells us, "but speaking the truth in love, we are to grow up in all aspects into ... Christ." What does this mean? That words of love can't truly help someone unless they are paired with words of truth.

Last week, Shawn was on "Instant Messenger" on his computer talking to several of his friends about problems he was having with his girlfriend. She just wasn't spending as much time with Shawn as she used to, and he was wondering if he should break up with her because of it.

Most of Shawn's friends said something like, "It'll be all right. She'll come around." Then finally, Eric went out on a limb and said, "You know, it's her first year of high school, and she's trying really hard to be popular. It's kind of changing her, and not in a good way. I know you like her, Shawn, but I don't think she's treating you the way she should." There it was: blunt, honest words of truth. Of course, the sender—in this case, Eric—should examine his or her heart and make sure the truth is told in a loving spirit. With that as a guide, the difficult information can be put to good use.

When you mix truth and love, the mixture becomes medicine for others. When you have love without truth, you've just got syrup. When you have truth without love, you have acid. Jesus was a great and loving truth-teller. He told the Pharisees they were a bunch of "vipers" for the terrible things they were doing, but he also mourned for them when they wouldn't see the truth (Matthew 23:33, 37-39). If a friend is being a jerk and expecting you to put up with it, ask God what it would look like for you to speak the truth in love.

Real Love Doesn't Preserve Relationships at Any Cost

Real love will risk the loss of a relationship if that's what it takes to love the other person well. Again, Jesus is our example.

A Pharisee invited Jesus over for lunch. Somehow, during the meal, a prostitute who had heard of the forgiving love of Jesus burst into the room, began weeping, and covered Jesus' feet with perfume. "She began to wet His feet with her tears, and kept wiping them with the hair of her head, and kissing His feet, and anointing them with the perfume" (Luke 7:38, NASB). How she loved him! The Pharisee missed the point, though. As he watched, he was thinking, "If this man were a prophet He would know ... what sort of person this woman is who is touching Him, that she is a sinner" (Luke 7:39, NASB).

But Jesus knew the man's type, so he turned to the Pharisee and said, "I entered your house; you gave Me no water for My feet, but she has wet My feet with her tears, and wiped them with her hair. You gave Me no kiss; but she, since the time I came in, has not ceased to kiss My feet. You did not anoint My head with oil, but she anointed My feet with perfume. For this reason I say to you, her sins, which are many, have been forgiven, for she loved much; but he who is forgiven little loves little" (7:44-47, NASB). Jesus is willing to risk his relationship with his host. He is not willing to hide the truth in order to look "nice." This is one of those healthy boundaries we talked about earlier in the book.

Real Help Insists Upon Accountability
If you're really going to help somebody, you can't put up with excuses. You don't need to be harsh, but you do need to draw the line.

Every time a rescue victim makes an excuse, he is inviting you to accept it—even if it's a poor one. As soon as you do, you've become part of his game. Letting him work his game is a very unloving thing to do. It is actually a kind thing to say gently, "That's not good enough. You can do better, and I expect more—I expect the best—from you."

Real Help Doesn't "Fix" Things
As we said earlier, when we fix things, we improve a situation for a friend without allowing him to learn anything. He gets

relief and gains no understanding. He says, "Whew!" You did all (or most of) the work, and it's likely the same situation will come up again. Guess who your friend will turn to? That's right. You.

Not long ago, eighteen-year-old Sam was at a party where two of his friends got drunk. Both his friends had cars, so Sam took away their car keys. The next day, both his friends were furious with him, but Sam might have saved some lives. He gave them real help because they had to face the inconveniences of getting drunk: walking home or spending the night in uncomfortable quarters. He didn't make things easy for them by letting them do what they wanted in the moment, at the expense of others.

Giving Real Help Means Going Beyond Your Comfort Zone

All of us have a comfort level we try to protect and preserve. Maybe we avoid conflict. Maybe we try to be what others want us to be. Maybe we are perfectionists. All these patterns help keep us comfortable.

When Sam took his friends' keys, he went beyond his comfort zone (he hates conflict). He was willing to do this, though, because he felt strongly that his friends shouldn't endanger themselves or others.

Getting out of your comfort zone may increase your stress in the short run, but in the long run, it'll free you from people who only want to use you to meet their needs.

Putting It All Together

These five principles are "moves" you can make to bust stress dramatically:

- speak the truth in love
- risk the relationship, if necessary
- insist on accountability
- don't fix things
- ditch your comfort zone when necessary

When you do this, you're announcing that freeloaders need not apply for your services. Those who simply want to loot the lives of others will recognize you're not an easy target. They'll tend to leave you alone and you can get on with being compassionate toward those who want real help.

Note of caution: I'm not saying that "freeloaders" aren't worthy of compassion. Certainly God loves people who use others for their benefit. The point is, you need to learn to recognize needy people who don't really want help, and save yourself the stress of pouring your life into the black hole of their neediness. Pray for them, that they'll "hit bottom," get into some constructive pain, and wake up to their need for real help.

You'll feel less stressed, and in time, so will they.

STRESS 101:

The sourcebook *Stress A-Z* reports that "Qualities most appreciated in friends include loyalty, trust, and an ability to keep a confidence. People want to feel that they can rely on their friends and can have an open and honest friendship during good as well as stressful times. When friends are supportive, they help relieve the stress during periods of turmoil or crisis."*

As we've talked about in this chapter, some friends are overly needy: they depend on you for things they really should be getting from God. Other friends will ask for things that are appropriate for you to give. It isn't always easy to know the difference, but as you ask him to, God will increase your wisdom. Which of your friends truly needs your support right now? Remember to pray for both types of friends, and to establish healthy boundaries for yourself as you support and love them.

* Ada P. Kahn, *Stress A-Z* (New York: Checkmark, 2000), 147.

Conclusion

Congratulations! We've come a long way, and you have done some serious stressbusting. But the journey isn't over.

For the rest of your life, you'll be facing stress. I hope that you'll take what you have learned from this book to help you along the way.

But if there is one thing and one thing only you take from this book, please remember this: God loves you, and he is with you in the midst of your stress, whatever it is. He will give you all the resources you need to face any trials he allows to come your way. Knowing this is the biggest stressbuster of all.

Guaranteed.

GOD ON STRESS:
"May the God of hope fill you with all joy and peace as you trust in him, so that you may overflow with hope by the power of the Holy Spirit" (Romans 15:13, NIV).

Notes

Two
Connecting With Others

1. The idea of safe people comes from Henry Cloud and John Townsend's book, *Safe People* (Grand Rapids, Mich: Zondervan, 1996).

Three
Getting Real

1. Arnold P. Goldstein and Ellen McGinnis, *Skillstreaming the Adolescent*, rev. ed. (Research: Champaign, Ill., 1997), 223.

Five
Knowing Yourself

1. Emil Brunner, *Man in Revolt* (Philadelphia: Westminster, 1947), 490.
2. Darrell Scott, with Steve Rabey, *Chain Reaction* (Nashville: Thomas Nelson, 2001), 5.
3. John Eldredge, "Wild at Heart" tape series, tape 1, Colorado Springs, Colo.: Ransomed Heart Ministries, 2000.

Six
Finding Rest

1. Paul Tournier, "Fatigue in Modern Life," in Paul Tournier, ed., *Fatigue in Modern Society* (Richmond, Va.: John Knox, 1965), 27.
2. Georges Crespy, "Fatigue and Rest According to the Bible," in Paul Tournier, ed., *Fatigue*, 67.
3. Richard Foster, *The Freedom of Simplicity* (San Francisco: HarperCollins, 1981), 58.
4. Paul Tournier, *The Whole Person in a Broken World* (New York: Harper and Row, 1964), 125.

Seven
Dealing With Confusing Adults

1. Earl Hipp, *Fighting Invisible Tigers*, rev. ed. (Minneapolis: Free Spirit, 1995), 95.
2. Hipp, 96.

Eight
Beating School Stress

1. Merle Fossum and Marilyn Mason, *Facing Shame* (New York: W.W. Norton, 1986), 70-83.
2. Fossum and Mason, 73.

3. P.A. Hauck, *Overcoming Frustration and Anger*, cited in Marilyn Miller, *Coping With Weapons and Violence in Your School and on Your Street* (New York: Rosen, 1993), 127.

4. Miller, 142.

Nine
Facing Family Stress

1. Maggie Scarf, *Intimate Worlds: Inside the Family* (New York: Random, 1995), 85.

Ten
Slaying the Perfectionism Monster

1. Judy Loken, *Teacher, I Can't Learn School!* (www.northern-lightsdesign.com/teacher).

2. Miriam Adderholdt-Elliott, *Perfectionism: What's Bad about Being Too Good?* (Minneapolis: Free Spirit, 1987), 11.

3. Adderholdt-Elliott, 22.

4. G. Abott-Smith, *Manual Greek Lexicon of the New Testament* (London: T & T Clark, 1937), 479.

5. Dave Shores, notes from sermon, "The Greatest Gift of All," delivered August 26, 2001.

6. Henry Cloud, *Changes That Heal* (Grand Rapids, Mich.: Zondervan, 1990), 195-96.

Eleven
Defending Your Beliefs

1. Daniel Allen Butler, *"Unsinkable": The Full Story of the RMS Titanic* (Mechanicsburg, Penn.: Stackpole, 1998), 115, 117, 146, 151.

Thirteen
Juggling Priorities

1. Milan Kundera, *The Unbearable Lightness of Being* (New York: Harper and Row, 1984), 41.

Fourteen
Coping With Troubled Friends

1. These first four indications that someone wants rescue, not real help, are based on Julia Cameron, *The Artist's Way* (New York: Tarcher/Putnam, 1992), 44-49.